THE PEOPLE DETECTIVE

Tom McGregor is the pseudonym of a well-known author, journalist and critic. Previously a television researcher, he has written several books on the film and TV industries. His previous books include *Saving Grace*, *The Making of Hornblower* and *Alan Bleasdale's Oliver Twist: The Official Companion*, which chronicled the making of the TV series in London and the Czech Republic.

Born in Scotland, he is a direct descendant of Rob Roy (hence the pseudonym). He now lives and works in west London.

THE
PEOPLE
DETECTIVE

Discovering Your Family Roots

TOM McGREGOR

HarperCollins*Entertainment*
An Imprint of HarperCollins*Publishers*

RDF TELEVISION

HarperCollins*Entertainment*
An Imprint of HarperCollins*Publishers*
77–85 Fulham Palace Road,
Hammersmith, London W6 8JB

www.fireandwater.com

This paperback edition 2002

1 3 5 7 9 8 6 4 2

First published in Great Britain by
HarperCollins*Entertainment* 2001

Copyright © Tom McGregor 2001

The author asserts the moral right to
be identified as the author of this work

By arrangement with the BBC
The BBC logo is a trademark of the British Broadcasting Corporation
and is used under licence
BBC logo © BBC 1996

This book accompanies the television series *The People Detective*,
made by RDF Media.com Ltd for the BBC
Executive Producer: Sam Organ
Series Producer: Jo Vale

ISBN 0 00 711722 1

Set in Photina

Printed and bound in Great Britain by
Omnia Books Limited, Glasgow

CONTENTS

ILLUSTRATIONS

The author and publisher are grateful to the following for use of photographic material:

The Trustees of the Weston Park Foundation, UK
Bridgeman Art Library
James Chalmers photographs reproduced from archive material of
    London Missionary Society/Council for World Mission
Devon County Council
Public Record Office
Ida Erasmus
Reproduction of the Ovaltine ad with kind permission of Novartis,
    legal successor of Wander UK
Hulton Getty

ACKNOWLEDGMENTS

I am indebted to many people without whose input and advice I could not have written this book. Professional genealogists Paul Blake, Steve Thomas, Sabine Meyer and Nick Barratt provided invaluable information and many anecdotes shedding light on the dos and don'ts of family history. Contributors to the series, Charlotte Sainsbury, David Gore, Ann Perigo, John Todd and Tracy Whitaker, shared their insights and personal experiences of being 'people detectives'. Hilary Hale steered me through the maze of records in the Family Records Centre and the London Metropolitan Archives. Production company RDF provided me with many research notes, and Windsor Herald at the College of Arms shed light on the arcane world of Heraldry. Many thanks to all the above.

Yet my greatest debt is to my publishers. I suspect I deserved a good smack on occasion, yet all I received was endless patience and good humour. So I would like to thank publisher Val Hudson, editor Monica Chakraverty and also Jo Wilson for their encouragement and support throughout this project.

Glossary of Terms

g.   great
FRC   Family Records Centre
GRO   General Register Office
PRO   Public Record Office
SOAS   School of Oriental and African Studies
SoG   Society of Genealogists

INTRODUCTION

As a museum curator, I spend a pleasurable part of my time helping people understand the past through the letters, objects and treasured personal possessions that have survived. Often the process is surprising (to put it mildly) and the past has endless secrets to reveal if you choose to look.

One of the most rewarding areas of investigation is family history, and I was delighted to have the opportunity to lead *The People Detective* onto Britain's TV screens. As well as meeting wonderful people and seeing exciting new places, work on the series revealed the ways in which our ancestors' experiences can bring to life the amazing stuff of history books. It also helps us understand who and where we are today. For all the people who followed in the footsteps of their ancestors it was an emotional and physical journey they will never forget!

But why embark on such a journey? Certainly, everyone in the series had very different reasons. For Charlotte Sainsbury, a ceramic restorer, it was a need to understand more about her ancestor, James Chalmers, who was tantalisingly marked on the family tree as 'missionary eaten by cannibals' ('and deservedly too' as one of Charlotte's relations pointed out!) The truth was far more complex than we could have imagined and the search took us from the sedate halls of a Cambridge college to the stormy seas of the China Straits and the remote island communities off the coast of Papua New Guinea.

Here, Chalmers and his wife, Jane, set out to bring Christianity to the local people but they brought much more besides; helping to end inter-village warfare and protecting the people from Empire carpetbaggers also formed part of their remit. Although held up as the ultimate Victorian missionary, Chalmers was anything but conventional. Hard-drinking and plain-speaking, he was admired by the people he worked with for his sensitivity. He opposed those who sought to destroy local cultures.

Sadly, Chalmers did meet a brutal end, killed and eaten by the people of Goaribari in 1901. In our travels, Charlotte was able to meet the descendants of his killers. Their community is still overshadowed by the death of Chalmers and they were delighted to have the opportunity to discuss the tragedy with his descendant. What we learned was a story of immense heroism and bravery that turned a faded name on a dusty document into the story of a man whose memory is still alive and well in the country where he worked and died. But it also revealed the harder edge of the British Empire and the cruelties of retribution.

For actor David Maybrick, finding out about his Victorian ancestors was a chance to unearth the facts of a terrible murder scandal that was still talked of in hushed voices by his own family. In the 1880s, Liverpool was rocked by the revelation that a respected cotton-trading family had skeletons in the cupboard so shocking that a murder trial resulted and a young woman was accused and found guilty of poisoning her rich, older husband. For David, the main motive of his enquiry was to discover whether his ancestor, Florence Maybrick, would have been found guilty of murdering her husband today. Visiting all the scenes of the alleged crime, and talking with experts in legal and forensic medicine, we came to the conclusion that Florence was a victim of a Victorian sexism that had shaped both trial and verdict. Whether she was guilty or not was quite another matter. She may well have had good reason to take to the poison bottle; David's final discovery was that the alleged murder victim (Florence's husband, James) is now thought to be the likeliest candidate for Jack the Ripper. As I said, history has surprises in store for all of us!

Sarah Apps knew only a little about her ancestor Claughton Pellew. Coming from a background where distinguished military and naval figures stud the family tree, it was perhaps no surprise that this artist and conscientious objector had been largely forgotten by his own people.

Together, we set out to unearth her talented and highly original ancestor. For Sarah, this was to be a real learning experience. As well as seeing photographs, reading letters and viewing paintings, Sarah got a chance to relive some of her ancestor's experiences. As a con-scientious objector in the First World War, Claughton suffered brutal treatment at the hands of the military authorities. He also spent long periods in prison. To understand this more fully, Sarah agreed to spend a whole day and night behind bars and to go through the prison regime of the day. This showed her that making a decision not to fight in the First World War needed a good deal of bravery and determination which did not quite fit with accusations of cowardice.

We ended our journey in Norfolk, meeting the people who knew Claughton in his later years. There, in the place where he lived and painted, Sarah came to the conclusion that she wished she had had the opportunity to know her once-forgotten ancestor, a man for whom art, principle and a love of nature were everything.

For boxer Spencer Fearon, knowing nothing about his ancestors was a real driving force. Coming to England from Jamaica in the 1950s, Spencer's parents had told him little about his past. As his mother said: 'Digging up the past can awake Zombies,' but that did not stop us! Our only way forward was to go to Jamaica and start our investigation by talking to Spencer's surviving relations and visiting the places where they lived. We also searched through the Island Record Office for documentary evidence.

As we expected, the journey gave both of us terrible insights into the slave trade and the living conditions of those who suffered under it. It also showed us the strength of those who chose to stand up to the system, and finally took us to a remote mountain village. Here, in the land called Cockpit Country, we heard the story of the Maroons. These were a people who escaped from slavery and, with limited arms and small numbers, maintained their freedom in the face of British aggression. On the hillside overlooking the village, Spencer was able to see the graves of his mother's family and to go through the ceremony of raising the ancestors with the present day Maroons. It was a chance for Spencer to glimpse an heroic past and to understand his own deeply rooted fighting spirit.

Glamour is not always something you expect to find in family history, but for Clare Cowley it was everywhere we looked! Clare had heard that her ancestor had been a model in the 1930s but knew little more than that. Fortunately, the *News of the World* archive and the History of Advertising Trust had information aplenty for us. So, on a bitter winter's day, we started our journey at a farmhouse, high in the Pennines. Here, Clare's ancestor Gloria (known by the press as 'the mystery mannequin') had been brought up by her grandparents. She was just plain May Kenworthy then and, after working as a winder in a local textile mill (putting wool onto bobbins), fled to Manchester to start a career on the stage. In following in Gloria's footsteps, Clare had a go at working the textile machinery and trod the boards, but the biggest challenge came in London. Here, Gloria (after being talent-spotted by Gordon Selfridge) took her first steps as a fashion model and here, too, Clare was put through her paces by one of today's leading deportment teachers.

For Clare, the experience revealed the hard work and determination that Gloria put into her transformation. Having set her sights on being top of her profession, nothing was to stop her. By the peak of her career, she had mingled with the rich and famous and become the most photographed woman in Europe. As an unexpected challenge, Clare was given the opportunity to model 1930s clothes in the luxurious surroundings of Claridge's. For both of us it was as if history had come alive, as well as providing a deserved tribute to the 'Queen of Mannequins'.

One story was different to the others. For many years I had been fascinated by the tale of Mary Bateman, the Leeds witch. Living and working in Leeds, it's a story that I still hear people talk about. Were there, I wondered, any descendants of this notorious lady? With the help of our research team we managed to track down Mary's great-great-great-great-great-granddaughter. And the most astonishing thing was she had no idea that her ancestor was so famous!

When I met Tracy Whitaker and her parents, I asked them what kind of an ancestor they hoped to have. Mr Whitaker hoped that it was Captain Cook. Tracy, on the other hand, hoped for someone who had done good work for society. Her only fear was that the person might have been evil or a murderer. Knowing that Mary Bateman had been tried and hanged for murder and implicated in a series of frauds, I was very worried about how Tracy and her family would deal with the facts. And for Tracy there was worse to come. Her ancestor's body had been used as a medical specimen and still survives in a museum in Leeds. So Tracy was able to meet her ancestor face-to-face! But, fortunately, there were no tears. Tracy is a student of forensic medicine and was fascinated to see Mary, if not in the flesh then certainly in the bone.

Throughout our investigation, Tracy constantly challenged the evidence that we unearthed. Was Mary such a bad person after all? Was she just a wise woman who accidentally poisoned one of her clients? Certainly, for someone trying to survive and bring up a family in Regency Leeds, life was hard and chances had to be taken when they arrived. Tracy brought home the facts of Mary's suffering and turned her from a fairytale character into a figure of sympathy.

The final revelation came with a reconstruction of Mary's face using the latest scientific technology. Would she look anything like Tracy? The answer to this was no, but we did get a chance to take Mary's skull on the train to London to be scanned. It was her first real trip to the metropolis and, I have to say, she was the strangest bit of hand luggage I've ever carried.

Travelling with so many people into the lives of their ancestors has been challenging and rewarding. I hope that the series and this illuminating book go some way to inspiring others to be their own people detectives.

Daru Rooke

GENEALOGY AND FAMILY HISTORY

Why Discover Your Family History?
✤
The History of Last Names
✤
Professional Genealogists

They Passed This Way

If you could see your ancestors, all standing in a row

Do you think you'd be proud of them, or don't you really know?

Some strange discoveries are made in climbing family trees,

And some of them do not particularly please.

If you could see your ancestors all standing in a row

There might be some of them perhaps,

You would not care to know.

But there's another question which requires a different view.

If you could meet your ancestors, would they be proud of you?

Anon

The professionals, experts and seasoned amateurs who have contributed to the *People Detective* series and to this book can offer invaluable first-hand hints to anyone interested in genealogy. No one, they agree, should approach their family's history in the confident expectation that they will be able to trace their line back to that magical date of 1066 – or even further. Professional genealogist and researcher Nick Barratt says, 'If you get further back than 1837 you are, frankly, doing pretty well' (1837 is the date when, in England, civil registration of births, marriages and deaths began). Civil registration began even later for the rest of the United Kingdom, so results before then may well be in the lap of the gods.

This is where it should be pointed out that the *People Detective* TV series, differs from the book because much of the research information had to be left out of the programmes so that they could fit into their half-hour slot. Researchers and producers spent months using myriad resources at various institutions in order to get hold of the material used in the series. Although not always shown, research was the backbone of the series – just as it is to genealogy in general – and no one should underestimate the amount of time involved.

But that doesn't mean research will be impossible for you to carry out privately. Rather, it is *difficult*. It means that you may have to travel to find out about your family. You may have to leaf through sources that, initially, may seem unlikely (probate inventories, maps, tithe records, hearth taxes). But what you will discover, if your researches are confined within the British Isles, is that you are exceptionally well served by the information available. Great Britain is unique: bureaucracy started – and started being recorded – with the Domesday Book in 1086. No other country has such a wealth of information about its residents over the last thousand years. If you try hard enough, and if you are lucky enough, you may well surprise yourself by how far back you can trace your roots.

Even if you don't get as far back as you had hoped, you may be able to move 'sideways' and discover what people were like, how they lived, what they owned and what disputes they were involved in. Countless surprises lurk here: some early eighteenth-century manorial records show, for example, that the poor in rural areas were more worried about the safety of their livestock than that of their children; the unpalatable yet incontrovertible point being that animals cost money to acquire and children are free.

Genealogy is exactly like peeling an onion: more and more layers are revealed as you go along. And if you're lucky enough to be able to trawl through the centuries with your ancestors, both they and the world they lived in will begin to come to life. As Nick Barratt says, 'Finding out what people were like is the fun part; it's where genealogy and family history come together. And it's what people are being encouraged to find out. What was their house like? What did they own? What was society like? Maps, estate records, expenditure records, records of legal disputes: there are endless sources of information that may answer these questions. A whole way of life evolves. Not just a list of names.'

Why Discover Your Family History?

The interest in genealogy has, over the last twenty years or so, become something of an epidemic. There are innumerable books on the subject and there has been a huge rise in genealogical and family history societies all over the world – but why? The experts cite no single reason, but share several theories. One is that we are no longer a society dominated by religion and that our search for our roots is something of a replacement for the security offered by the church. Another is that we reckon we were really rather grand in the past. This, however, is a pretty dangerous notion to harbour and can lead to disappointment or downright disgust. Any genealogist will tell you that you're quite likely to encounter poverty, crime, illiteracy and duplicity in the realm of your ancestors – see, for example, the chapter on Mary Bateman, the Yorkshire witch! Yet it's still extremely common for people to imagine they're related to aristocracy or royalty. As Steve Thomas of Achievements, a genealogical research company in Canterbury, says, 'Quite frankly, if you're aristocratic you're already going to know about it. Too many people imagine they're going to uncover some sort of grandeur and, when research uncovers an illiterate peasant instead of a duke, they simply won't believe it. I know of instances of people using one genealogical firm for assistance and then, when they're told the results, they go to another, hoping to find something different; they never do.'

Yet people still persist – sometimes to an astonishing degree. Steve Thomas recalls an American who spent a great deal of money purchasing a gold ring, the (missing) documentation of which, when found, would prove that the ring had belonged to King James I and that its current owner would have precedence over Prince William in the line to the British throne. It is true that this is one of the more outlandish stories you'll hear, but it's symptomatic of the craze for seeking out blue blood.

Even those *with* blue blood have harboured delusions of even greater grandeur. Monarchs the world over have traditionally boasted descent from deities – and England is no exception. In the Long Gallery at Hatfield House, a pedigree of Elizabeth I is on display, showing her supposed family tree all the way back to Adam. It is, unsurprisingly, splendidly vague.

Another, simpler reason why people embark on genealogical research is to find out, geographically, where their forebears came from – and this is one of the most satisfactory areas of research. If you're successful, you'll end up secure in the knowledge that you 'belong' to a particular place. You'll also conjoin family with local history – often a source of deep satisfaction and great interest.

One of the other reasons most commonly cited for research is the breakdown of the family unit. Unlike many of our Victorian ancestors, few of us belong to families of ten siblings and a vast extended family. We're more likely to be a 'nuclear' unit and, furthermore, one that has geographically, financially or emotionally distanced itself from other relatives – especially during the past century.

Perhaps the most likely reason is one that is echoed by Jo Vale, producer of *The People Detective*: 'I think, really, people who are interested in their family trees have this sense that there's something *missing*. Something intangible that will give them a greater sense of self as well as a history personified.' This, certainly, was the case for Spencer Fearon, whose black ancestry *The People Detective* helped uncover, although not, as was initially hoped, back to Africa. Jo Vale is quite frank about that: 'Oh yes, we hoped to get back beyond his West Indian antecedents to Africa, but that's the whole thing about genealogy: records disappear, people die, events go unrecorded ... we had literally *hundreds* of stories proposed to us for the series. But most of them fell by the wayside for the same reason: it's incredibly difficult to prove, for certain, who your ancestors were.'

The History of Last Names

In the maze that is genealogy, people often assume there is one constant, reliable factor to help them with their family search: their surname. Unfortunately, this assumption is completely erroneous. Surnames, like family trees, can take the most unexpected twists and turns and can lead you down paths you didn't know existed. Over the centuries, they have been modified or even altered beyond recognition by such disparate factors as local dialect, intonation, a shaky grasp of the written word and – very commonly – complete illiteracy. The last variant is something that professional genealogists warn people about: almost without exception, people will encounter illiterate ancestors in their genealogical researches. Some people refuse to accept the fact that their forebears couldn't write, and that denial doesn't, of course, make sense. At some point in the distant past, *none* of us could write.

The need to be identified by a name stretches back to antiquity. The ancient Romans were the first to evolve a complex system of names that, though disappearing with the fall of the empire, was in many ways comparable to our own present system. At its most sophisticated, the Empire used four names: one to indicate the individual, another to link that individual to the clan, a third (effectively, our surname) to indicate the various divisions of the clan and a fourth (not always used) to indicate specific qualities of that person. This system didn't survive the collapse of the Empire and, for hundreds of years, people were generally identified by one name alone.

The practice of attaching a second name that would pass from father to son re-emerged in Venice, where the first surviving record of people with surnames dates back to AD 982. The custom then spread to France, England, Germany, and on to most of Europe. While the exact date of using surnames in England cannot be pinpointed, their use in aristocratic circles arrived with the Norman Conquest and started to become commonplace in the late thirteenth century. As William Camden wrote in *Remaines of a Greater Worke Concerning Britaine* (1586):

> *About the yeare of our Lord 1000 surnames began to be taken up in France, and in England about the time of the Conquest, or else a little before, under King Edward the Confessor, who was all Frenchified ... but the French and wee termed them Surnames, not because they are the names of the sire, or the father, but because they are super added to Christian names.*

It is worth noting that, in present-day French, the word *surnom* actually means nickname, whilst what we call a surname translates as *nom de famille*. This linguistic difference provides something of a clue to the origins of surnames. Broadly, they evolved from four different sources: from a person's relationship with a parent; from a place of origin; from an occupation or from a nickname or characteristic. Thus, respectively, evolved the names Johnson, Field, Carpenter and Redhead.

That's the potted version. Surnames are the double-edged sword of genealogy: while it's their very existence that enables us to trace our family history, their propensity to change for myriad different reasons can make life difficult for the family historian. As Richard McKinley, leading authority on the subject, has concluded: 'The development of hereditary surnames in this country was a prolonged and complex business, not operating uniformly over the whole of Britain, but subject to marked regional variations and to differences between one social class and another.'

Furthermore, if someone changed profession or moved location, their name often changed as well. When one John Ellis moved to Myddlewood in Shropshire in 1581, his neighbours called him Ellis Hammer, after the village he had come from, and his descendants adopted the Hammer surname.

In other parts of Great Britain, the picture is slightly different – and even more complicated. In Wales, for example, the use of fixed surnames wasn't commonplace until the sixteenth century and even, in remote parts of the country, the late eighteenth century. Traditionally, the Welsh had used the prefix 'ap' or 'ab' to denote 'son of'. Unification with England under the Tudors spread the use of English surnames – but also muddied the genealogical waters. William ap Robert, for instance, would have become either William Probert, or William Roberts.

In Scotland – where the equivalent for 'ap' was 'mac' – research into surnames is even more difficult due to the clan system. Traditionally, clan members adopted the name of the chieftain whose protection they sought, so there is no reason to suppose that if your name is MacDonald you are related to the chief of the clan of that name. And if your surname is abbreviated and spelled McDonald, you can forget the notion (and it's a common one) that you are descended from a bastard son of a chieftain: 'Mac' and 'Mc' are simply variants in spelling.

In many ways, research into surnames in Scotland and Wales is made more difficult by the fact that there were relatively few names. And then there are anomalies that make life even more awkward: like the outlawing in 1603 of the MacGregors because of their bloodthirsty reputation. The name was not permitted again until 1775. In Ireland, there's a bastard rumour attached to 'Fitz', and it's a widely held misconception that this prefix denotes illegitimacy. The fact is that it derives from the French *fils de* and means precisely that: 'son of'. The rumour of illegitimacy arose after Charles II chose to prefix the surname of several of his bastards with 'Fitz'.

Probably the most widespread reason for surnames changing is variations in spelling. In 1538, when Thomas Beckett, Henry VIII's chief minister, introduced parish registers, this was the first time many families had their names recorded in writing. Many of them were illiterate and would have spoken their names to a parish clerk. He would have written down what he heard – which was not necessarily the same as what they meant. Furthermore, there was no standardisation in spelling for the next three hundred years until the advent of compulsory education. This was theoretically in place before 1891, but was only actually implemented in that year, when government funding made it possible to provide free elementary education for all children. Add to all this the fact that one parish clerk may have interpreted names in a different way to his predecessor, and you are left with no reason to doubt that, in theory, the same person could have been entered in a parish register under two different names.

The fact that ancestors sometimes lied is another bane in the life of a genealogist. While people regularly lie about their age, many have also lied about their names – or indeed changed them on a whim. In England, you could change your name without any formality whatsoever; deed poll of change of name was sometimes enrolled in Chancery after 1851, and from 1903 in the Supreme Court of Judicature. But prior to the mid-nineteenth century, most changes of name went entirely unrecorded.

Surnames, therefore, are a far from simple subject, but an immensely interesting one. And they can lead into other elements of genealogy which professionals and amateurs alike find so rewarding. In the sleuthing process, you may well find yourself becoming acquainted with local history, maps, manorial records and other documents in order to trace your family. And so surname traces become part of the broader and increasingly rewarding subject of bringing your ancestors back to life.

The Petyt Surname

One story that was researched but not televised for *The People Detective* concerned two brothers, William and Sylvester Petyt, born in the 1630s in Yorkshire. They both rose from extremely modest means to become highly influential and very wealthy London lawyers. Their lives were extremely interesting – and so is the possible origin and subsequent development of their surname. For Petyt has many variants, including Pettie, Pettie, Pettee, Petit and, in Ireland, Pettitt. It is quite probable that the name may be of the 'nickname' origin, having originally been attributed to someone who was short of stature – from the Old (and Modern) French *petit*.

On the other hand, the name may well be of Scottish origin and could derive from a place. The name may indicate 'one who came from Petty', a place in Inverness-shire. And the name of that place itself could derive from the Gaelic word 'peit', meaning a share or portion of land. The earliest record of the name in Scotland is from 1296, when it is mentioned that Johan Petyt of the Miernes, Lanarkshire, rendered homage. The name disappears from records until 1395, when a Master Duncan Petyt was archdeacon of Glasgow.

The earliest record of the surname in England is found in 1198, when one William Petie is recorded in the 'Feet of Fines', Nottinghamshire. In 1249, one Walter le Petiet is mentioned in the 'Assine Rolls' of Wiltshire and Thomas Petyt is listed in the 'Subside Rolls' of Leicestershire in 1327. The descendants of William and Sylvester Petyt have kept that spelling of the name, although the most common variant is now Petit.

An area of genealogy relevant to tracing surnames, and one that is growing in popularity, is the One-Name Study. It's a fairly specialised area, but one that can yield fascinating results. Basically, anyone conducting a one-name study is embarking on a project researching all occurrences of a surname – not just their own family members bearing that name. The Guild of One-Name Studies is the place to start here. Anyone with an interest in one-name studies can become a member, although to register you have to be interested in studying the worldwide occurrences of your name. Your study may concentrate on aspects such as geographical distribution and changes thereof over the centuries, or tracing the genealogy of as many lines as possible bearing the name. The great thing about one-name studies is that you'll find enormous numbers of people willing to co-operate: collaborative efforts between people studying the same name (even if they're just doing their own family) can reap enormous rewards as regards discovering new relatives.

There are hundreds of publications relating to surnames, and countless sites on the internet. An interesting recent development is MyMap™, software developed by Oxford Ancestors research company, which maps out the current geographical distribution of any surname. The maps present the precise locations of individuals with the same name, revealing, for instance, local clustering around the historical origin or significant dispersion events. It's a real bonus for researchers into one-name studies, but is also interesting for all family researchers – even those with a common name.

A fantastically useful source of information for private research on living relatives is a CD-ROM called the *UK Info Disk*, which includes everyone in UK telephone directories and electoral registers. Going slightly further back in time, if you know the rough area where your antecedents lived, old phone books are also incredibly useful and can be located in local libraries.

Professional Genealogists

If you haven't the time or inclination to travel in order to track down ancestors with the same surname, you may think about calling in a professional. After all, *The People Detective* did, even though they had several researchers of their own. One of the reasons for this was the sheer volume of people who contacted the series with stories of their ancestors. As series producer Jo Vale is at pains to emphasise, it was essential to prove beyond the shadow of a doubt that the descendants participating in the series were the blood relatives of the ancestors featured. This may sound like a rather obvious point, but it's one that is vital, and not easy, to establish. If you're going to work backwards from yourself, you'll find that, six generations down the line, you'll have found sixty-four g.g.g.g. grandparents. And if you're going to work forwards from one of those ancestors, there is no mathematical equation to follow. The sky (or perhaps sixteen children) really is the limit: you can't have more than two blood parents but you can have any number of children.

Most of the *People Detective* stories are the results of professional genealogists working forwards from the likes of Mary Bateman and the Maybrick family, down to individuals who are descended from them. Most genealogists stress that this is the 'wrong' methodology for genealogy; that you must work backwards from yourself. Yet sometimes it is the only way to operate. It's not uncommon to 'lose' an ancestor somewhere along the line, leaving you with the options of either abandoning your family researches or taking the risky route of looking for someone who appears 'likely' a generation or two above the person you've lost. This, in the main, was the problem faced by the *People Detective* team: looking for likely descendants. (True, they had the added complication of finding a descendant who wanted to appear on television ... but that's television for you.) 'Yes,' says Jo Vale, 'we were effectively doing the opposite of normal genealogy but, on the other hand, a lot of people embark on family research because they think they're descended from someone famous. So, in reality, we were doing the same as a lot of other people.'

Just as some people privately hire professional genealogists, Jo Vale did the same for *The People Detective:* 'We simply didn't have the resources to research hundreds of stories,' she says. ' If, for example, someone came to us who thought they were the descendant of someone and had, say, a copy of that person's marriage certificate, we would need to find the children from that marriage, which would mean having to look all over the country for birth certificates within ten or fifteen years of that marriage. Or, indeed, before that marriage: being born out of wedlock isn't exactly a modern phenomenon. Although our researchers became pretty adept at the basics of genealogy, it really doesn't make sense to use a TV researcher to try to prove family histories.'

So, whether you're researching forwards or backwards, a professional will be able to help. So why do relatively few people employ experts to help them? The most obvious reason is a financial one: while genealogists don't have set charges for a particular project, most will quote hourly or daily rates. The former range from about £5–£30 and the latter usually start at £100. But the main reason why people tend to research their families themselves is, principally, because they enjoy it. Another reason, as we have seen, is that people are put off by the truth: if they think they're descended from the aristocracy they're not going to relish being told by someone else that they're as ordinary as the rest of us.

Not that genealogists themselves have always been squeaky-clean. By common accord, the nineteenth century is regarded as the golden age of bad genealogy, when an increasing number of families rose from nowhere and applied a portion of their vast fortunes to genealogists who 'traced' their aristocratic ancestries. This practice muddied the genealogical waters for years, and it wasn't until 1968 that the first professional body – the Association of Genealogists and Record Agents –

was formed to establish a code of practice. But one can't apportion all the blame to Victorian parvenus: the reason why the College of Arms was set up in the fifteenth century was because newly-rich families were using coats of arms to which they weren't entitled.

Given that it is now easy to find a reputable genealogist, what are the benefits of using one? Advice, specialised skills and speed are the main reasons. Any genealogical company worth its salt will have microfiched copies of any data available at the major public institutions (census returns and records of births, marriages and deaths since 1837, for example). What's more, it'll have its own library. And, perhaps more valuable, years of practice means that it's likely to have an answer to any question – no matter how peculiar.

At Achievements research company, I asked how I might go about tracing my great-grandfather, about whom I know absolutely nothing beyond his surname; I didn't even have a clue where he had been born. When pressed to elaborate on this stunning lack of information, I remembered that there was supposed to be a statue of him in some town in Queensland. That was enough for Steve Thomas to instantly suggest contacting the Queensland Office of Public Works (or equivalent body), and enquiring about what statues were erected when. I could then get in touch with an Australian newspaper library about the unveiling of the relevant statue; no newspaper in the area would neglect to mention the erection of a statue. Furthermore, a newspaper article would reveal my ancestor's dates of birth and death, and probably much more besides. A very useful start to tracing a relative I thought I would never learn about.

One of the most useful specific skills that most professional genealogists have is a familiarity with Latin and an ability to read old handwriting. If you're delving into the early 1700s and beyond, you're almost certainly going to encounter documents written in Latin. For a professional like Nick Barratt, this isn't a problem: he has a degree in thirteenth-century history. But for amateurs, a document written in an ancient language in an unfamiliar script is going to be almost impossible to transcribe. An extreme example of peculiar (but not Latin) writing was found by a client of Achievements in the needlework basket of a deceased aunt. Inside was a long strip of milliners' tape with words in both English and French. After some study, a few names were deciphered, revealing the identity of the wife of a French marshal. Subsequent research revealed that the tape had been sewn into the rim of a maid's crinoline skirt and conveyed news and military intelligence between Brussels and Paris during the Franco-Prussian war of the 1860s. Not your everyday story, then.

A professional can also be employed to do everyday, mundane genealogical research. This doesn't mean you'll paint yourself out of the picture: he or she can get on with the donkey work while you pursue rather more interesting areas. What, after all, is the fun in trawling through general registration indexes looking for someone with a fairly common surname in order to find their birth, death or marriage certificates?

So where do you find a professional? Many advertise in publications such as *Family Tree* magazine – but be wary; the magazine itself may be respectable, but the advertisers may not be. However, anyone advertising in the Society of Genealogists' own magazine is required to have been a member of that society for more than five years, or to be a member of the Association of Genealogists and Record Agents. Even that doesn't mean they're necessarily brilliant, so your best bet is to contact the Association of Genealogists and Records Agents direct. Alternatively, contact a research company such as Achievements in Canterbury, where the researchers are trained at the affiliated Institute of Heraldic and Genealogical Studies, and which holds copies of most records available to the general public as well as unique indexes of its own.

Further Information

Professional researchers
Achievements
79–82 Northgate
Canterbury
Kent CT1 1BA
Tel: 01227 462 618
Fax: 01227 765 617
www.achievements.co.uk
e-mail: achievements@achievements.co.uk

Association of Genealogists & Record Agents
29 Badgers Close
Horsham
West Sussex RH12 5RU
For a list of reliable genealogists and record agents, send a £2.50 SAE (UK) or 6 IRCs (overseas)

Association of Scottish Genealogists & Record Agents
PO Box 174
Edinburgh EH3 5QZ
www.asgra.co.uk
For a list of reliable genealogists and record agents working in Scotland send a first-class SAE (UK) or 2 IRCs (overseas). Alternatively, the list is published on the web site.

Association of Professional Genealogists in Ireland
c/o The Honorary Secretary
30 Harlech Crescent
Clonskeagh
Dublin 14
Eire
www.indigo.ie
For reliable genealogists and record agents in Ireland, send 2 IRCs.

GOING IT ALONE:
Practical Information

How to Begin
❧
Wills
❧
Genealogy and the Internet

How to Begin

If genealogy were easy and an exact science, there would be no need for the hundreds of books, myriad organisations and hundreds of thousands of web sites dedicated to the subject. Apart from the fortunate few (usually aristocrats) who can trace their line back hundreds of years, the rest of us are entering unknown territory when we embark on genealogy. Which is where guidance is invaluable. Genealogist Steve Thomas is unequivocal about his first piece of advice: 'It's vital to pay attention to what your living relatives have to say. So many people just don't bother and could save themselves a lot of time and energy if they did.' Elderly relatives reminiscing about the past may not be everyone's idea of fun, but it could pay enormous dividends. And oral history, by common accord, is the essential starting point for anyone researching their family history.

Nick Barratt, who used to work at the Public Record Office (PRO), elaborates on this: 'Often people ignore the present; they don't work with the known and then go backwards. This can lead to someone finding a name from, say, two hundred years ago, recognising it as a family name, and assuming it's an ancestor. The likelihood is that it's not.'

Given that the PRO is the country's most important source of statistics relating to genealogy, it's worth taking further advice from that quarter. 'What I would highly recommend,' says Barratt, 'is for any researcher to attend one of the – usually monthly – induction courses at the PRO. They last a day, they're free and they take you on a tour of the office, offer advice on main sources of information and on how to get started. Too many people come unprepared to the PRO and think they can pull a record of their family off a shelf. It's not like that at all. You have to know what you want, identify it, order it and then interpret it. Alternatively, there's an annual one-week (non-residential) summer school which you pay for and that goes beyond the basic introduction and includes lectures on various aspects of family history, including use of the internet.'

Either way, it does seem wise to familiarise yourself with the basics of the PRO. Given that the institution has around one hundred million documents occupying 172 kilometres of shelf space (adding roughly two to three kilometres every year), learning by instruction rather than by your mistakes is by far the most sensible option.

The internet, touted in some (ill-advised) quarters as the catch-all answer to genealogical enquiries, also serves a function here. Yet there is a caveat: the PRO's site contains document descriptions, but not document *content*. There are plans to put content on-line, starting with the 1901 census (census returns, by law, are unavailable to the public for one hundred years), but on-line content of other records is still a long way off.

Another piece of advice from the PRO is that people should be aware that they will be dealing with documents that are not specifically designed for family history. The methodology employed by all genealogists dealing with the nineteenth and twentieth centuries – namely checking general registration (births, marriages and deaths), census returns and parish records – is not a failsafe mechanism for corroborating earlier family histories. Other avenues may need to be explored and, as Barratt says, 'People should be aware that they may end up looking at documents that were not designed as aides to family history.' These might include anything from probate inventories to hearth taxes, maps, tax records, manorial records and Exchequer inquisitions. Furthermore, any official document that predates 1733 is likely to be written in Latin. So, not only will you be dealing with strange handwriting, but you'll also be tackling an unfamiliar language. True, the documents cited above may seem incidental to family history, but they are sometimes the only sources through which one can trace one's antecedents. Also, they make for fascinating reading ...

Civil Registration

If, like most people, you decide not to use the services of a professional genealogist, you'll need to be aware that civil registration of births, marriages and deaths started in England and Wales in 1837, in Scotland in 1855 and in Ireland in 1864. Certificates can be obtained from local register offices or the GRO (addresses are at the back of the book). Research in Ireland can pose a real problem for family researchers, as vast numbers of civil registration archives and parish records were either routinely destroyed or lost in a fire in the Public Record Office in Dublin in 1922. Other sources can fill the gaps, but any professional would strongly advise you to read one of the many books exclusively covering Ireland. Wherever you are in the British Isles, it's important to remember that you should start tracing your ancestry by looking at your *own* birth certificate; it is not unheard of to discover surprising information there.

Census Returns

After civil registration documents, your next step should be to look at census returns. Modern censuses began in 1801 and were taken every ten years, except during the war in 1941. All are available at the FRC, although a hundred-year ruling prevents public access to later ones. The first three returns are, frankly, fairly patchy, but the 1841 census gives names, occupations and approximate ages. In 1851, relationships, dates and places of birth were added. So, if you find your family on the 1841 census, then look them up again on the 1851 return: if they hadn't moved, there may be more information there. Be prepared for inconsistencies and inaccuracies, though; people didn't always tell the truth.

Until the 1881 census, you need to already know your family's address in order to search a census return (addresses are on birth, marriage and death certificates). But the 1881 census – the most useful of all – has an index which covers the whole of England, Wales and Scotland. It's available as a CD-ROM and can be searched in a number of ways. Again, Ireland is the exception here: the ruling on disclosure of personal content is different and the 1901 and 1911 returns are already available. For the rest of the country, 2002 will be a busy year as regards family history, as this is when the 1901 census becomes available – on-line as well as on CD-ROM.

Parish Registers

The next port of call will generally be parish registers – and this is when research can start to become unwieldy. Church of England parish registers were started under the orders of Thomas Cromwell, Henry VIII's Vicar-General, in 1538 and have been kept ever since – although during the Civil War and Commonwealth (1649–60), many were not maintained. These record baptisms, marriages and burials and are the primary source for this material until 1838. By no means all of them have survived, although most from the late sixteenth century onwards are available in county record offices and on the GRO indexes. The Society of Genealogists (SoG) publishes a National Index of Parish Registers, describing the location of surviving parish registers up to 1837.

Parish registers have altered throughout the centuries, but the basic information has remained the same. It is essential to note, however, that they record *baptisms* and not births, *burials* and not deaths. You can be pretty certain that burial followed swiftly after death, but don't assume that baptisms occurred shortly after birth. It's a modern myth that people baptised their children days or weeks after birth because of high infant mortality: it was, in fact, common practice to have several of your children baptised at the same time. It's also worth noting that some people didn't receive a Christian burial and so any record of their demise has to be found elsewhere. *The People Detective* has an example: Mary Bateman, the Yorkshire witch, was denied one.

After 1754, marriage registers should – but don't always – include the signatures or marks of the spouses and their witnesses, and this is where some people become rather miffed, as they discover their ancestors were completely illiterate. As far as professionals are concerned, this is par for the course.

Other Sources

If civil registration, census returns and parish records fail to divulge the secrets you're after, then you'll have to broaden your search into an almost infinite variety of areas. This can be incredibly frustrating but also enormous fun and hugely satisfying from a historical perspective. You may find yourself looking, as the *People Detective* team did, in some highly unexpected areas, or unearthing unexpected documents in some areas. In researching the story of Claughton Pellew, for example, researcher Vicky Greenly found herself looking in the archives of the Tate Gallery, and she uncovered a wealth of letters and other personal memorabilia. The story of Gloria, the 1930s supermodel, took researchers to such places as the History of Advertising Trust archive and the Gaydon Heritage Motor Centre. Research into Mary Bateman led to Thackray Medical

Museum and the Old Operating Theatre Museum. None of these places are 'official' ports of call for genealogists, but they're examples of how the trail to your ancestors can lead you into weird, wonderful and sometimes completely unknown places.

Some of the more interesting research sources require little effort to discover, and can be incredibly interesting. And some, like photographs, are probably already in your possession. Most of us have old family photographs featuring people we can't identify, and some of them may date as far back as the 1840s, the advent of portrait photography. And they can divulge plenty of secrets that could help you with your family research. The name of the studio where the photograph was taken may lead you to a new town or city (most pre-1900 portraits were taken in a studio), and, if the portrait was taken outside a studio, the houses in the background may provide a clue to a date or location. Photographs of people in military uniform can be highly revealing, as can the clothes of civilians: they can help with giving you an approximate date.

Newspapers

Another potentially superb source of information is that of newspapers. It will help you a great deal if your ancestors were high-profile people; however, with increasing literacy in the Victorian era, more and more daily trivia about ordinary individuals began to be printed. *The Times* is the only national newspaper indexed from its early days (at its – unindexed – earliest, it was called the *Daily Universal Register*, assuming its current name in 1788). Issues dating from 1790–1908 are on CD-ROM at the British Library Newspaper Library, the SoG and other reference libraries.

The British Library Newspaper Library in north London has the largest collection of newspapers in the country, including London newspapers from 1603–1800 and news sheets from 1641–60. The library also holds the widest collection of Irish newspapers. The various newspapers are fantastic resources for information on court cases, bankruptcies, deaths, sensations and anything else of note on a national and local level. Other good libraries for newspapers are the Bodleian in Oxford and the National Libraries of Ireland, Scotland and Wales.

Local reference libraries are also well worth visiting to see what you can find. In *The People Detective*, for instance, much information about both Mary Bateman and Florence Maybrick was found in newspapers in the libraries in, respectively, Leeds and Liverpool. Newspapers are fabulous sources for finding out about criminal trials: court transcripts are not necessarily available, whereas newspaper coverage will carry the same information – usually with much more background.

An excellent publication is *Local Newspapers (England and Wales) 1750–1920*, published in 1991 by the Federation of Family History Societies. It lists which local papers are available and where they are held. A good port of call on the internet is www.earl.org.uk/magnet/, a site that details where and how to find magazines, journals and newspapers in libraries.

Maps

Another genealogical area you will undoubtedly come across is cartography. Maps from many different eras will help you build up a picture of where and how your ancestors lived (the *People Detective* story about Spencer Fearon, for example, made good use of maps in trying to locate his ancestors.) Maps can also prove invaluable in finding other records. Ordinance Survey maps, for example, started in 1805 and the larger ones are detailed, accurate, and can reveal the location of buildings that no longer exist. Earlier maps are another area of genealogy that proves fascinating. The earliest maps were made in the 1570s and, much like the maps of today, they were sold as information sheets to travellers. Maps dedicated to roads started being published in the late seventeenth century, and large format county maps began to appear in the middle of the eighteenth century. Local libraries, museums and record offices generally have lists of maps, past and present, of their locality. The PRO also has a vast collection of maps in its library and in the Map and Large Document Room.

Probably the most intriguing maps are those that were made by local landowners for their estates, which therefore include information you are unlikely to find elsewhere. Boundaries, hedges, fields and dwellings are marked and, vitally for the family researcher, the name of the tenant or owner is indicated too. This is a prime example of using documents that were not created for genealogical purposes in order to trace your ancestors. In general, nearly all records, from before parish records started in 1538, were kept for the purpose of detailing the activities and possessions of the wealthier members of society. But they can, often by chance, reveal information about our humbler ancestors. These maps were kept to show the amount farmers paid towards maintaining the church and clergy, and they can be extremely revealing. It is largely a matter of chance about what survives of estate and enclosure maps, however, tithe maps were rationalised in 1836 and are very well documented at local record offices and the PRO.

Nonconformist Records

One of the reasons why you may not be able to locate your ancestors by using parish registers is that they may have been Nonconformists. These Protestant denominations, which dissented from the Church of England, include: Baptists, Quakers, Methodists and, latterly, Mormons.

Finding records of Nonconformist ancestors won't be easy unless you are aware of the denomination to which they belonged. If you do, however, have this information, you'll find that most congregations (generally meeting in a chapel or meeting house rather than the parish church) kept their own registers of births, marriages and, after 1691, burials. It was this date that saw the passing of the Toleration Act, allowing Nonconformists to set up their own burial grounds. Prior to that, the dead had, in theory, to be buried in the local parish churchyard. In practice, parish priests considered Nonconformists to be unbaptised and many refused to bury them.

Records of Nonconformists can be located in a variety of sources. Quakers kept their own registers and indexes, now held at the library of the Religious Society of Friends. The PRO has a wide variety of differing denominational material while Scotland, Ireland and Wales hold much information in national libraries and Public Record Offices. If you have internet access, you'll find links to Nonconformist web-sites at www.cyndislist.com

This has been a very brief summary of some of the major sources you may use in tracing your family history; the sky really is the limit and you're likely to find yourself looking in the archives of organisations you didn't even know existed. But that's the fun part of genealogy, or at least genealogy in Britain. Spare a thought for family researchers on the Continent. In Germany, for example, a certificate is regarded as a highly personal document, not a public record, If you want to research a family, you have to have written authorisation from a court, solicitor, or family member. Furthermore, there is no central record office of national archives (like the PRO), but a separate record office in every town and, in big cities, there may be several.

In Germany, there is also no luxury such as being able to view old parish registers at your leisure. If you want documents from before 1874, you have to write to the church registrar office in order to get information – and you have to know where the person you are looking for was born or lived and whether they were Protestant or Catholic. Another difficulty is that many church registers from parts of Germany that are now in Poland have been destroyed, although there is a church archive in Berlin containing some records, but for Protestants only. A lot more records were destroyed in the war and are no longer available. It is difficult, for example, to obtain pre-1945 certificates from parts of Hamburg, and virtually no records survived the Allied bombing of Dresden.

Wills

Professional genealogists agree that wills are an endlessly fascinating source of information. Finding out how an ancestor wished his or her belongings to be distributed after death can yield intriguing insights into family history. A will may tell you the name, social status, residence and occupation of the deceased, and names and relationships of the executors and the beneficiaries. Its contents may also tell you a great deal about how an ancestor lived. And a will may often be the only personal document left by your ancestor.

Yet for most of us wills are comparatively modern. Before the twentieth century, a lot of people, especially women, didn't bother leaving one, despite the fact that, as far back as 1540, the Statute of Wills allowed for males over the age of fourteen and females over the age of twelve to leave one. A will written by a lunatic, traitor, prisoner, heretic or slave was invalid. And if someone died intestate and had property to leave, the dispersal of the estate was decided in court by a process known as 'administration'. If they had only possessions to leave, the court generally didn't get involved. Nowadays, the composition of the deceased's family decides how the estate is divided if someone dies intestate.

Wills written after January 1858 are extremely easy to access. The Probate Act of the previous year required that all wills be registered with the Principal Probate Registry. Copies of all wills from that date are held there and you can access them. Alphabetical lists of wills can be accessed from various other sources, including the Society of Genealogists. Wills in Ireland are held at the National Archives in Dublin and, in Scotland, at the National Archives of Scotland and individual Sheriff Courts. However, there is a detailed index to wills, called the *National Probate Calendar*, which is more widely available (at least up to 1943). This gives the date of death and usually more information as well. It can be seen on microfiche or microfilm, at the PRO, the Family Records Centre (FRC), the SoG and the Guildhall Library, London.

Before 1858, you are not going to find any centralised collection of wills. The probate of any will in England and Wales was granted at any one of over two hundred and fifty ecclesiastical courts throughout the country, where the executor was empowered to act on the deceased's wishes. You will therefore need to know roughly the geographical area where your ancestor may have died, as well as the approximate date of that death. There are, however, various collections of indexes of wills and, again, the SoG is probably your best bet. The records of only one court, the Prerogative Court of Canterbury, can be seen at the PRO and FRC. Ecclesiastical courts had no jurisdiction over bequests of freehold property so, if bequests of such property led to dispute, the case would revert to Chancery or Common law. A terrific guide to church courts and their records is *Probate Jurisdictions: Where to Look for Wills* by J. Gibson, published in 1994 by the Federation of Family History Societies.

There are potentially major problems associated with pre-1858 will searches. Apart from finding the court that heard probate, you have to ascertain where its records are kept. And finding the court itself isn't just about locating the area but about deciding which level of ecclesiastical court you're looking for. There were various types, of which the lowest, the archdeaconry court, usually dealt with the will of a person of small means. If someone had goods or property in more than one archdeaconry, the will would usually be dealt with in a superior court – that of a bishop or an archbishop.

The Petyt Brothers

Locating wills prior to 1858 is far more complicated, but can also be great fun and highly rewarding. In researching the story of William and Sylvester Petyt, who are mentioned in the previous chapter, the *People Detective* researcher, Nick Barratt, found wills and legacies of the two brothers, which were extremely detailed and informative, at the PRO. Sylvester, for example, states that he wishes to be buried ten feet deep between three and four o'clock in the afternoon ...

It was, says Nick Barratt, 'one of the most fascinating pieces of research I've ever done. A really great story – mainly because of the brothers' rise to prominence and the wealth of documentation about them.' The story touched on several fascinating areas, including the history and etymology of their surname (see previous chapter), the legal system in London in the late seventeenth and early eighteenth centuries and, most fascinating, on the wills and legacies of the rich. The Petyts weren't born rich; they were two of the ten children born to a yeoman farmer in the hamlet of Storiths, near Bolton Abbey in Yorkshire. They attended a local 'dame school', where they gained a basic education that enabled them to attend Skipton Grammar School and then went to London to train as lawyers. William went on to gain fame and a certain measure of notoriety by publishing, in 1680, three controversial books on the Rights of Parliament. He subsequently – and pertinently to this book – was employed during the reigns of William III and then Queen Anne as Keeper of the Records, sorting out the national records, which were then housed in the Tower of London. He died in 1707.

Sylvester stayed within the law and became Principal of Barnard's Inn, one of the Inns of Court in London. He made a vast amount of money and, on his death in 1719, left £30,000 – today, the equivalent of about £2.5 million. Sylvester's will and inventory makes for a terrific historical document, of interest to any family researcher, even if the language is often extremely arcane. Parts of both are reproduced below.

The Last Will and Testament of Sylvester Petyt (Signed on the 23rd May, 1719)

I Sylvester Petyt of Barnards Inn, London Gent. Being of sound mind and good health revoking disclaiming all and every the Will and Wills and Testaments by me at any time before made do make publish and declare this for and as my last Will and Testament in manner following that is to say I give my Soul unto the hand of God relying wholly upon his free grace and mercy for the pardon of all my sins and for the fruition of everlasting peace and blessedness through Jesus Christ my only Saviour. My body [... illegible ...] to be buried if I die in London or within twenty miles thereof in the churchyard of St Andrews Holborn side of the church there, ten foot deep at least but if I die above twenty miles from London then to be buried in the churchyard where I shall so die ...

Sylvester then goes on – at enormous length – to itemise his bequests. He appears to have been something of a money-lender, because numerous legacies are prefaced by words along the lines:

I do forgive unto my niece Elizabeth now the wife of Richard
Wright and to the said Richard Wright all such sums and sums
of money which now is or are shall be due and owing by and
from them or either of them unto me at the time of my death.

The sheer number of people mentioned in the will makes perusal of it worthwhile for anyone whose antecedents were even remotely connected to Sylvester Petyt. After all, it was written at the beginning of the eighteenth century, when documented information about people was pretty sparse. Paragraphs like the following provide vital clues that may not be found in other sources:

I do acquit Robert Hudson of Settle who married Isabelle the
daughter of my niece Farrand of and from the debt which she
oweth me and I do order and direct that he have his bond
delivered unto him to be cancelled and I do give unto the said
Isabelle twenty pounds to be paid unto her or her husband
within one year next after my death.

Other information refers to family relationships, possessions and even the whereabouts of residences. For example:

I give to my cousin Mr Christopher Petyt of Outon in
Westmorland fifty pounds to be paid to him within two years
after my death and I do give unto the saide Stephen Catterson
the pictures of my brother and myself which were or are in my
late bedchamber in the house in Bell Savage Yard and also my
long swing clock in the next room to my said bedchamber which
was my brothers which said two pictures and clock I will shall

be sent to Skipton and placed in the library there in the church...

... I do give unto my worthy friend Peniston Lamb of
Lincolns Inn Gent my diamond ring which I usually wear set
with seven diamonds ...

Because he was so well known, Sylvester Petyt's life was pretty well documented at the time, and indeed afterwards (he has a long mention in the *Dictionary of National Biography*). Had he been unknown, however, phrases such as the following could provide vital clues for the family researcher:

I do give unto the church wardens of the Parish of St Andrew
Holborn in London and Middlesex wherein I have lived ever
since I came to London ten pounds to be distributed by them
amongst the poor there.

This one sentence is enough to send the genealogist straight to the records of the Parish of St Andrew, in search of more information.

Petyt's inventory, c. 1720, is a goldmine as regards recreating a picture of his worldly goods and the life he led. A copy if it can also be found at the PRO. Selected entries include the following:

A true and perfect particular inventory of all and singular the
goods chattels and effects of Silvester Petyt late of Bernards Inn
London Gent. Deceased begun to be taxenvalued and appraised
the 19th November 1719 and continued by several
adjournments to the 11th January following.

By virtue of a commission of appraisement approved, hosted
and issued out of the Prerogative Court of Canterbury and

*divested unto us whose names are hereunto subscribed as
follows viz.*

*4 silver buckles, 3 bits of silver, 2 buttons, one carved gilt cup
and cover, 2 tankards, 2 salvers, 2 pottingers, 3 candlesticks, 1
plate, 1 sugar box, 1 cup, 2 tumblers, 3 castors, 1 cup and
cover, 1 soup ladle, 20 spoons, 12 forks, 1 salt, 1 scoloptd
sugar dish, 3 seals, 2 pairs of buttons, 11 ounces of old silver
coin all weighing 338 ounces and quarter all 5s. d. per ounce.
total: £88.14.6*

*100 King Edwards shillings.
total: £5*

*one diamond ring with 7 stones
total: £12*

*a fashionable silver watch and chain
total: £3*

*a tankard and salt and 2 spoons old sterling all weighing
25 ounces and 4 pennyweight at 5s. per ounce
total: £6.11.0*

*24 old shillings
total: £1*

*in money paid into Mr Lambs hands
total: £5.15.1*

a piece of old gold
total: £0.8.6

combined total: £1400.14.2

The testator's pictures, household goods and wearing apparel
viz.
82 old pictures of different sizes
total: £3

Mr Petyt's and Mr Caterson's pictures in oval gilt frames
total: £1.1.0

194 large and small prints, maps and coats of arms
total: £1.10.0

7 prints frames with glass and 1 Dutch glass, 2 oval prints of
Queen Anne and Prince George in carved frames
total: 15s.

an Indian card table lined with crimson plush, 1 walnut tree
inlaid table, a small table and tea board, a writing stand, 1
walnut tree filligree table and 8 stands
total: 15s.

the pictures of the Earl and Countess of Cumberland and their
daughter in black and gilt frames
total: £1.10.0

two pictures of Mr William Petyt and one other of Mr Silvester
Petyt in gilt frames
total: £3.3.0

Securities by Mortgage, viz:
1715 April 6
An indenture 5 partite between Sir Francis Molineaux Bart.
and William Draper Esq of the 1st part, the Lady Viscountess
How widow and executrix of the late Lord Viscount How and
mother and guardian of the present Lord Viscount How (then
an infant) of the 2nd part George Golding Esq of the 3rd part
Sir Thomas Gorvy Kt (then one of the masters of the High
Court of Chancery) of the 4th part and the testator of the 5th
part purporting to be an assignment of a mortgage of certain
lands and hereditaments in Langar in the county of
Nottingham for the remainder of a term of 200 years for
securing to the testator £2000 principal money and interest at
the rate of 5% / year and whereon all interest is endorsed to be
paid to the 17th April 1718 principal money
£2000

As you can see, the will and legacy of Sylvester Petyt make for fascinating reading, whether you are a descendant of his or not. They also provide an interesting and unique insight into aspects of early eighteenth-century life. Such discoveries remain invaluable for helping to visualise what life was like for people in that era. To help you search for your own ancestor's will, a list of useful addresses appears at the end of this chapter.

Genealogy and the Internet

Because genealogy is so labour-intensive, there is an enormous temptation to take what seems like the easiest route, which for many people is the internet. Such is the proliferation of genealogical information on the web that you could spend months with your mouse. But be warned; as professional genealogist Paul Blake says: 'The internet is wonderful as a finding aid; as a source of where to go to for information. But if you use it as proof of genealogy, you're in danger of huge inaccuracies. The real problem is that you don't know who's done the research. The people who input the information may be Joe Public or an expert: you simply don't know. People shouldn't rely on indexes. They should always refer back to the original sources, or copies and microfiches of those sources.' The current problem is that any information found on-line will not be a representation of original material: it will have been transcribed by someone.

This does not, however, mean that the internet isn't useful – and it certainly doesn't deter millions of people from using it as a genealogical gateway. It is estimated that genealogy sites are the second most visited on the internet (pornography is the most popular) and, at the time of writing, a search on the word 'genealogy' revealed that there are 1,306,903 web sites relevant to the subject. That's an awful lot of genealogy. Most of it is US-based and a lot of it is, frankly, useless.

But given the extraordinary role of the internet in genealogy, the rapidly increasing numbers of people going on-line and the temptation to use the web as a one-stop shop for your ancestors, it's worth considering the medium as the most accessible source of genealogical information. So, if you're one of the increasing numbers of family historians with a computer, have a look at the internet. Not because you will necessarily find concrete information about your family, but because it's a sensible place to get a feel for genealogy without having to leave your desk.

Here are the sites recommended by the experts. But remember: without exception, every professional emphasises that the internet is a 'finding aid' and that any actual records you see should be checked against the original sources. Using the internet is, however, extremely useful for finding organisations to help you. Furthermore, you'll find people to help you as well: it's a fabulous way to make contact with other family history researchers and to send messages anywhere in the world. Join a mailing list or a discussion group and you may find that someone else is researching the same family or topic as you. Genealogy is, after all, about people – and there are millions of them out there.

The best place to start with British genealogy on the web is GENUKI, the Genealogical Information Service for the UK and Ireland (www.genuki.org.uk). It contains basic general information on family research in the British Isles and provides comprehensive links to every other useful web site on the subject. Highly recommended.

Cyndi's List (www.cyndislist.com) has some 65,000 links to other sites and also to software suppliers. If you're going to make serious use of the internet you could do with family tree programs – Family Tree Maker and Generations are the best – to enable you to put your results on your PC.

FAMILIA (www.earl.org.uk/familia) carries a list of libraries in the UK and the resources they hold. It also has maps providing useful information on place names and boundary changes. And it links to:

The Public Record Office (www.pro.gov.uk), where every information leaflet published by the office can be viewed or downloaded. This makes for an invaluable resource as you can pretty well establish if documents you want to look at – no matter how obscure – are stored here.

The Society of Genealogists (SoG) (www.sog.org.uk) also has extremely useful information leaflets. A charity whose objects are to 'promote, encourage and foster the study, science and knowledge of genealogy', it's Britain's main family history organisation. A selection of its key records and indexes are being put on-line at: www.origins.net

The Commonwealth War Graves Commission (www.cwgc.org.uk) has an on-line database where you can type in the name of a deceased and the place where they died, and a search will locate their date of birth and the names of their next of kin.

Of the searchable on-line databases, the Mormon site (officially, the Church of Jesus Christ of Latter-Day Saints) is the most talked-about. Located at: www.familysearch.com and officially copyrighted as IGI (International Genealogical Index), it houses the largest genealogical collection of its kind in the world. And you don't need to be on the internet to access it. It has over 3,400 branches, or Family History Centres, in seventy-five countries which hold microfiches of the information available on-line. And that's something of a clues to how vast this organisation is. At the time of writing, its database includes 35.6 million lineage-linked names and over six hundred million names in total. The question that most people ask, however, is why adherents to an obscure religion in Utah would be interested in compiling a database of our ancestors? The answer is that they're not: they're interested in *their* ancestors.

Here is why. The Mormon church believes in a divine plan of happiness that enables family relationships to be perpetuated beyond the grave. Sacred ordinances and covenants available in holy temples make it possible for individuals to return to the presence of God and for families to be united eternally. The Saviour, the church contends, taught that everyone who has ever lived on earth should have the opportunity to hear his gospel and receive the ordinances of salvation. Dead people can receive these ordinances from worthy church members of the Mormon faith. So, in a nutshell, the faith believes in uniting families for all eternity. The Gospel Principles go on to say that: 'Families should also compile and write the information they find about their ancestors. Then this information can be used by all family members.'

It is a tribute to the Mormon faith that, in the above context, they include non-believers as 'family members'. Most of the information they have gathered for what is effectively the baptism of their ancestors is available free of charge to the rest of the world. But while the IGI index is a fabulous research tool, it is also flawed, and it is essential to check any information found against original sources. This is both for reasons of human error when inputting data and because some of the information submitted may be based on little more than educated guesswork.

While most of the entries on the index are transcribed directly from sources such as parish records (at the time of writing, they have two hundred and forty cameras microfilming records in nearly forty-four countries), others are from information deposited by families conducting their own research and may be unsubstantiated by any official documents. As genealogist Steve Thomas says, 'You have to look at the index very carefully and note which are extractions from registers and which are submissions from individuals.' There are, on the site, different letters and symbols to denote the provenance of each entry.

The real library in Utah, as opposed to the virtual one, is something of a genealogical Nirvana and, astonishingly, receives an average of 2400 visitors a day. Its collections include over 300,000 books and 4500 periodicals. It also has an extensive collection of original records. Sabine Meyer, a genealogist working in Eastern Europe, has an example: 'After 1945, Poland sold a lot of Protestant church records directly to the Mormons. Poles are Catholics and they decided they no longer wanted the Protestant registers.'

Further Information

Wills: National Sources
For London and for information on regional Probate Offices:
Principal Registry of the Family Division
Probate Search Room
First Avenue House
42–49 High Holborn
London WC1V 6NP
Tel: 020 7936 7000

Scotland (for wills up to 1985)
HM General Register Office
HM Register House
Princes Street
Edinburgh EH1 3YY
Tel: 0131 535 1352

Scotland (for wills after 1985)
HM Commissary Office
Sheriff Court House
27 Chambers Street
Edinburgh EH1 1LB
Tel: 0131 247 2850

Ireland
Republic of Ireland Probate Office
Four Courts
Dublin 7
Tel: 00 3531 888 6174

MARY BATEMAN,
the Yorkshire Witch

Witchcraft Through the Ages

✤

The Perigo Family – Tales from a Family Researcher

✤

Was Your Ancestor a Criminal?

> Our ancestors are the last people I should chose to have a visiting
> acquaintance with.
>
> Sheridan, *The Rivals*, 1775

Mary Bateman (née Harker) was born in 1768 in Aisenby,
Yorkshire, the daughter of a highly respected local farmer. Yet
Mary's own respectability was a veneer, behind which lurked a
world of witchcraft, 'cunning people' and extortion, culmi-
nating in her execution, in 1809, for murder. Her life story
caused a sensation at the time, became the subject of a book
and helped keep alive the myths and terrors about witchcraft
that persist to this day. It is apt, and spooky, that the *People
Detective* team recreated her physiognomy by means of laser
mapping and 3D-computer graphics, thus marrying modern
techniques to ancient superstitions.

The book, published in 1870 and snappily titled *Extraordinary Life and Character of Mary Bateman the Yorkshire witch*, wastes no time in informing us that:

> *At five years of age, Mary Bateman began to display a knavish and vicious disposition. At that age, she stole a pair of morocco shoes, and secreted them for some months in her father's barn; at length she brought them out and pretended she had found them, but an enquiry proved that this was only one of those fraudulent devices which so strongly marked her future life.*

The book continues in this splendidly bombastic way, informing us that she grew up to be: 'a thief, a witch, and a smooth-tongued deceiver' and that her

> *frauds and barbarities ... will live when her person is forgotten, and will damn her name to everlasting fame, operating as a warning, not only to the present but to future ages, to shun the practice and detest the deceptive art of fortune-tellers.*

It is true that Mary Bateman's 'frauds and barbarities' live on, but rather than operating as a warning against witchcraft, they and other similar tales merely serve to heighten interest in the subject. And although, to most of us, witchcraft is regarded as something of a joke that gets an airing every Hallowe'en, it is still taken extremely seriously by certain sections of the population. Which is why it makes a fascinating story, and why finding a descendant of Mary Bateman made for such compelling television. Tracy Whitaker, the descendant in question, said that her worst fear about unearthing her family history would be discovering that she was related to someone evil. Her fears, then, were confirmed.

Or were they? Here are the bare bones of Mary Bateman's story. In Leeds, in 1778, Mary began to supplement her income as a dressmaker by advertising that she had supernatural powers. Charismatic, extremely charming and adept at identifying people's psychological weaknesses, she had little difficulty in convincing gullible friends and acquaintances of her aptitude for making love potions and for fortune-telling. Furthermore, she was skilled at exhorting money from individuals to help pay for solving their problems or arranging their futures.

In 1803, her reputation and position as a psychic rose further when she ingratiated herself with Joanna Southcott, a prominent prophet and psychic who visited Leeds that year. Southcott had a national reputation and profited greatly from her powers of prediction. She also had a talisman 'seal', which she sold for a guinea a time, claiming it was a ticket to heaven! She sold fourteen thousand of those seals to people who believed her claims – one of which was the notion that she was pregnant with the Second Christ, and another being that Armageddon was due in the year 2004. Impressed by Mary Bateman, Southcott succumbed to her flattery and personally 'sealed' her with her talisman; an action that conferred Mary with considerable clout as a prophet and healer.

In 1806, Mary claimed that her hen had laid an egg with 'Christ is coming' inscribed in its shell. She 'proved' this by inviting people round to witness the unfortunate hen laying more eggs with the same message: a message she had inscribed herself on previously laid eggs and which she reinserted into the hen. This alleged, ghastly performance merely served to heighten her stature and, combined with her saintly demeanour, make her much in demand. She became increasingly expert at tricking people out of money, and her hunger for financial gain even led her to poison two Quaker sisters and their mother and drove one young woman to an abortion and another close to suicide. At her trial, it emerged that her victims didn't go to the police because they feared her supernatural powers.

Mary's undoing started when, later that year, Rebecca Perigo and her husband William came to seek her help, having been told by a country doctor that Rebecca's 'flacking' breast was due to the fact that there were evil spirits at large. How right they were. Over the next two years Mary fleeced the Perigos of their entire savings and, in 1808, gave them a curative powder that resulted in Rebecca's agonised death from poisoning. Mary was arrested, tried for murder, and subsequently hanged.

Yet Mary persisted with her claims of innocence to the bitter end and she dressed in white for her hanging because, supported by her followers, she maintained that an angel would descend and remove her from the gallows. Twenty thousand people turned up to witness the spectacle, and there was said to be an eerie silence and supernatural glow at the time of her death.

The angel, however, failed to materialise to the assembled throng; whether or not it appeared to Mary is another issue. Many believed it had, and people paid to see her body and the pious expression she wore at the time of her death. Afterwards – and not very piously – her skin was sold in strips to ward off evil spirits and rich women paid to see eminent surgeon William Hey conducting a public dissection of her body. The dissection was part of her punishment. Bodily resurrection and an ascent to heaven were denied to her. There was no Christian burial and her bones remain, to this day, in the Thackray Medical Museum.

All in all, a gruesome little tale, related with gory relish in the transcript of her trial in 1809. But whilst Mary's claims seem ludicrously unbelievable to contemporary readers, they seemed less so within the context of the day, and against the background of belief in witchcraft.

Witchcraft Through the Ages

Vicky Greenly, who did much of the research on the Mary Bateman story, found the progression of belief in witchcraft particularly interesting. 'Belief and fear of witches was at its peak in Europe in the seventeenth century – the time of the notorious witch trials. Although trials had been going on since the fourteenth century, they were particularly vicious, especially in Germany, in that period. England,' she adds, 'was actually the least hairy place for witches.'

This was true with regard to the method of their execution: in England, witches were hanged and then burned, while in Scotland and the Continent they were generally burned alive. This didn't, however, prevent the English witch hunts from being assiduous: in the seventeenth and early eighteenth centuries; some forty thousand witches – mostly women – were murdered during the great hunts. Their crimes ranged from being a spinster, to having warts, to ergot poisoning (ergot is a fungus, inducing convulsions and hallucinations in anyone who eats it).

Political interest in witchcraft was nothing new – in the eleventh century King Knut (Canute) was frightened enough of the subject to issue anti-witchcraft laws – but the hell, fire and brimstone hurled at anything that smacked of witchery was primarily fuelled by the church. As Vicky Greenly discovered: 'It gave the church fantastic control, especially at a time, the seventeenth century, when the country was politically and economically unstable. Basically, the church's take on it was that if you thought someone was a bit dodgy, you could accuse them of being a witch. It was also a way of seeking revenge against other members of your local community – and a method of trying to explain the inexplicable in a time of limited scientific and medical knowledge. But by the seventeen hundreds, there weren't so many witch trials. The country was more stable politically, the Age of Enlightenment had arrived and the grip of the church wasn't quite so tight. What's more, parliament started questioning the realities behind witchcraft.'

The questioning led, in 1736, to the passing by Parliament of the Witchcraft Act, which declared that witchcraft was no longer a criminal act. This invited something of a conundrum in some quarters: could an Act of Parliament decide such a thing? Amongst others, the Act was deemed to be a heinous assault on Christianity. People who held by the literal truth of the Bible, which so clearly stated the existence of a supernatural evil, were livid, claiming that the Act was contrary to the express laws of God.

The debate raged on, generally amongst the country's elite, but for the majority of the population the effect of the Act was to diminish interest in witchcraft and magic, at least in their popular manifestations. Instead, attention shifted to related supernatural beliefs: mainly spirit possession and other such diabolical phenomena and, later, fortune-telling. Which is where Mary Bateman and Joanna Southcott come in. They were exemplars of the eighteenth-century re-emergence of 'witches' in the guise of men and women who, in the main, ministered to broken hearts and neighbourhood grievances. That Mary was a con-artist of the first order is beyond doubt; that she was possessed of powers other than duplicity is highly unlikely. But the 'witch' tag remains, notwithstanding the fact that she was actually arrested for fraud and convicted of murder – both brutally prosaic crimes that have nothing to do with the supernatural.

It was not until the passing of the Fraudulent Mediums Act in 1951 that the concept of witchcraft in all and any of its manifestations disappeared from the statute books. That Act, effectively repealing the Witchcraft Act, enabled witches to exist again. And exist they do. According to the Pagan Federation, there are currently ten thousand initiated witches in this country. The witch religion, called Wicca (the Anglo-Saxon word for witch), was only founded in the last fifty years and now has an estimated million adherents worldwide; and none of them believes in the devil. Cassandra Latham, whose tax return states her occupation as 'professional witch', has stated that her job involves dealing with life's usual problems of relationships, jobs, money and health and that 'it's pastoral work, just like the vicar, really. Except that we use magic – like most religions.'

Yet the fear lives on, sometimes to a hysterical degree. At the time of writing, two US states (Kansas and Colorado) have banned the Harry Potter books on the grounds of promoting witchcraft. They do, however, celebrate Hallowe'en. One can only conclude that they view Hallowe'en as a legitimate commercial exercise and harmless Harry as an invitation to dance with the devil...

Further information on witches and witchcraft can be found at the Museum of Witchcraft in Boscastle, Cornwall. Fifty thousand visitors a year traipse through its doors and proprietor Graham King (a scientist by training and previous profession) says he believes in witchcraft because he has seen it work. The Harry Price (not Harry Potter!) Library at the University of London has an excellent archive on witchcraft. Harry Price was a psychic investigator in the 1920s and 30s who sought to expose fraudulent mediums and clairvoyants. The Folklore Society at the Warburg Institute, London, is also a mine of information, and its address can be found listed at the end of this chapter.

The Perigo Family – Tales from a Family Researcher

Ann Perigo from Yorkshire, whose husband is a descendant of the hapless and startlingly gullible William Perigo, has long been researching the Perigo family tree – and has some fascinating tales to tell. Both she and her husband appeared in *The People Detective*, but Ann's interest in genealogy stretches far beyond her family's connection with Mary Bateman: 'Quite frankly, if you're a Perigo or you're related to one, you're very likely to know about the connection with Mary Bateman. It's not often one of your ancestors is murdered by a witch ... But it was the strangeness of the Perigo name that led me to research

60

them. I'd already done my own family and they were pretty easy because they never moved; they were always in Yorkshire. The Perigos were far more complicated.'

It is a commonly held belief that the Perigo name is a Huguenot one, principally because of its obviously French origin. Ann, however, has traced the English Perigos further back than the first major Huguenot influx of 1572. 'The Perigos originally came into England, in Sussex, during the reign of Henry VIII. There may well have been Perigos who came in later, but I've traced the name back to the early sixteenth century.' The king, apparently, was preparing for war against France and wanted the best gunsmiths around and they, paradoxically, were to be found in France. He brought large numbers of them into the country, where the name Perigo was first recorded in the Denization Rolls. These, located at the PRO under Patent Rolls, are records of early immigrants who were unable to afford naturalisation and who therefore petitioned to the crown to become denizens, which gave them most of the rights enjoyed by a citizen. (Their children would automatically become citizens.) Indexes of denization after 1509 have also been published by the Huguenot Society.

In these Rolls, Ann found a record, dated 1544, of one John Perigo (written as 'Perago') and, intriguingly, he was recorded as having already been in the country for thirty years, having 'six children, English born'.

It appears that the Perigos were forgers (of the metal variety) and brought the charcoal-fired blast furnace with them from France. 'I'd always thought the English had invented it,' recalls Ann, 'but now it appears it was the French. After Sussex,' she continues, 'the Perigos and other forgemen seemed to have gone everywhere in groups; they probably had their own customs and language. And, as demand for cannons and guns diminished they moved up the country through Gloucestershire, Monmouthshire, Shropshire, Derbyshire and then into Leeds. They always seemed to be forgemen of some sort; cutlers in Leeds – that sort of thing.' The one who went to Leeds is the individual from whom all the Yorkshire Perigos (like William and Ann's husband) are descended.

So how did Ann discover all this? 'I didn't know about the Sussex connection until I read a wonderful article about French iron-working immigrants in Sheffield. The author reckoned they all originally came from Sussex – and he was right. We went down to Chichester and looked in the Record Office. What was extraordinary was that we found a whole village full of Perigos. I'd never heard of the village before and the Perigos mentioned were not on the IGI [Mormon] index. And that's why I'd say the IGI shouldn't be trusted: it's extremely useful but you've always got to check against the originals. Not that Mormon researchers had made any mistakes there – they simply hadn't looked at and recorded those records. We found a Perigo will from 1606 as well. That was absolutely lovely to see.'

But Ann hasn't yet conclusively traced her own branch of the Perigos beyond 1667 and is still trying to find a connection to the John Perago mentioned in the Patent Rolls. Lack of space precludes an exhaustive account of her researches, but here are a few of the problems – and triumphs – she has encountered. All are of relevance to the family researcher.

'It was no problem tracing back from my husband's family to the Leeds area as there were – and still are – lots of Perigos around. But then I lost them when I was looking for a certain

William Perigo (William is an incredibly common Perigo name) and couldn't find him anywhere. I knew he was born in Derbyshire in 1686 and knew that he'd married a Hannah Trickett, but I couldn't find the marriage certificate. Then, on the IGI, I found a "Guillemus" Perigo who had married Hannah Trickett. I'd been so used to looking towards the end of the alphabet for a William that I'd forgotten to look for a latinised version of the name.'

Names and variations thereof have been a constant source of Perigo problems for Ann. 'I've seen it written as Perago, Perigaux, Perigord, Perigo and Perigault. The most extreme example was when I was looking for Perigos in Sheffield in 1881. I knew they were there because I'd read about them in trade journals, but they weren't on the 1881 census. Eventually I found them under Periss! The original "g" and "o" must have been rounded, both looking vaguely like the letter 's' to the person who transcribed them. And then you've got to remember that a census recorder probably didn't think a name could end in an "o".' But the problems weren't limited to the Perigos: Ann couldn't find the Laurence family, who married into the Perigos, and who should have been included in the 1851 census. She tried Lawrence – and eventually found them listed as Lorence.

'Misspelling has always happened – and it always will happen,' says Ann. 'People record what they hear, and can make mistakes about what they see. That's why, the further back you go, the more trouble you're in. If you're looking back from 1538 you're quite likely to come to a dead end unless you can find your ancestors in taxation of settlement records. I've recently contacted the Derbyshire Record Office to ask about the areas I'm interested in, and they have quite a lot of settlement records. What's more, it looks like the forging industry in those areas may have started earlier than I'd thought.'

So does that mean Ann may find a link to the 'Sussex Perigos'? And is she going down the route of trying to tie the Sussex branch to the north of England branch? 'Yes. If you reach a dead end – which I have in 1667 in Sheffield – it's worth trying to tie-up two different branches. Someone in Sussex is working back from the original John Perago and I'm still trying to find a link between his family and the Yorkshire and Derbyshire Perigos. If we can match someone in between, then we will be on to something. But it's not helped by the fact that so many Perigos were called William. More unusual names are generally far better clues – most names tend to repeat themselves within families and the more unusual the better.' The problems at the Sussex end, however, are compounded by the fact that two John Peragos were listed in 1544. One was the man recorded as having six British-born children: the other as being an immigrant from France. 'What we don't know,' says Ann, 'is whether it's a duplicate entry, whether one John is the son of the other or even the grandson.'

A further problem was e-mailed to Ann when she thought she might have found a possible link, via a William Perigo (yes, another one) to Sussex. An e-mail from a fellow family-researcher informed her that he thought he'd found that William: and that he'd gone to America and was shot in some sort of native riot. Ann was horrified. 'He's the only William I've got who looks like he could link Derbyshire to Sussex – you can't let him be shot!' But he may well have been. The link may never be established. And that is something all genealogists must be prepared to come to terms with.

Was Your Ancestor a Criminal or a Member of the Underclasses?

Be prepared. You may be squeaky-clean but there is no guarantee that your ancestors were. After all, three of the *People Detective* stories involve people who spent time in prison, and some of your ancestors may have done so as well. Or they may have been deported. Genealogist Steve Thomas says: 'There are cases of people being deported for stealing a piece of coal. Terrible – yet terribly revealing as well. That piece of coal says it all, doesn't it? Someone only stole it because they were freezing to death; the coal itself represents the Industrial Revolution and the punishment reflects our expansion to territories overseas.' Another example of genealogy revealing a slice of life at that time.

Steve Thomas has also discovered the punishment for a certain Edward Dench in the 1600s: 'He was tried for petty larceny – I can't remember what he stole but it was something incredibly small. His punishment was to be whipped on a cross in a Cambridge square on two successive Saturdays.' This example illustrates that, while we consider imprisonment to be one of the most obvious forms of punishment for convicted criminals, this was not so in the past. The word 'prison', in fact, was only coined in 1823 when houses of correction and county jails were amalgamated and regulated by justices of the peace and, in 1877, by the National Prison Commission. Prior to that date, most criminal offences were punished by death or by a fine and/or whipping and, from the seventeenth century, by transportation.

Transportation was initially to America, and, consequently,

the image of voluntary colonisation ('plucky pilgrims'), or colonisation by default (mainly Irish and Scots with no hope of making ends meet at home) is a simplistic one. After the American Revolution, sentences of transportation were still passed, but convicts were held in prison instead. To ease overcrowding, temporary prisons were constructed in old ships, or 'hulks', moored in domestic coastal waters until a new penal colony – Australia – was developed. The first convicts were sent there with the First Fleet in 1787. Transportation ceased in 1867, although the sentence itself was only abolished twenty years later.

Whilst no one could feel anything but pity for an ancestor deported for stealing coal, other criminal cases may induce revulsion or laughter, or possibly both. 'The PRO is still waiting,' says Nick Barratt, 'for someone to come in looking for the naval ancestor who was court-marshalled for, according to Admiralty Records, "offences with a goat below deck". He was convicted and executed and the poor goat had its neck cut for complicity in the affair.' Quite how the unwitting descendant will react may never be discovered, but there's a serious side to Barratt's reference to the episode: it is used in staff training at the PRO as an example of how both staff and customers have to prepare themselves for anything.

Having a criminal in the family can, however, be quite good news for a genealogist. Historically, law-abiding people who led fairly mundane lives and were not part of a grand family didn't feature very much in records. They may even have slipped through the net altogether. But if they broke the law, the chances are that they left a trail. But where?

There are innumerable sources for tracing criminals, but the good news for the family researcher is that you're unlikely to be looking for a criminal ancestor just for the hell of it. You're most likely to embark on this route because the individual you're searching for doesn't appear in census returns, parish records or records of the armed forces and seems to have vanished. You will, therefore, be operating within a known timeframe and, probably, area.

Most counties in England had some sort of jail by the thirteenth century, to hold debtors and people awaiting trial. Houses of correction, established in 1575, held criminals, the homeless and even unmarried mothers. This last, shocking fact becomes even more appalling when one learns that unmarried mothers were treated abysmally until, in some cases, well into the twentieth century. The *People Detective* research team was told one life story about a woman, now in her seventies, who was brought up in a workhouse. Her daughter approached series producer Jo Vale, hoping that the team would be able to find out something about her mother's family, about whom she was totally ignorant. She knew that her grandmother had been in an asylum for the insane but, beyond that, she knew nothing.

'We really, really tried on that one,' says Jo Vale. 'We went through all sorts of records: parish records; Barnardo's; the other organisations that exported children at the beginning of the twentieth century. We were looking in the Winchester area, but some of the records there had been flooded, which didn't help. The family was Catholic, so we had a Catholic priest helping us as well. Eventually, he found records of the brothers and sisters of the woman in the asylum. They had all been baptised, and they had all died prematurely. To the priest, it was something of a triumph: they'd been baptised so they had gone to heaven. But for us it was a really bad day. We had to tell this woman that her grandmother may have been put into a lunatic asylum because her brothers and sisters had died and there was no one to look after her and her child. It was awful in one way – but at least she found out.'

A sad story and a really unpleasant reminder of how hard life was not so very long ago. Unmarried mothers were, to society at large, little better than criminals. No sophisticated system of justice would imprison an unmarried mother, but it didn't (and still doesn't) take much to have someone certified as insane. The end result is the same: they vanish from society. So, too, did other ailing ancestors whose families couldn't afford to care for them. Asylums, hospitals and workhouses were the only options available to them. Records of asylums and hospitals, however, are kept confidential for a century, so you'll only be lucky in locating an ancestor in such an institution if you're looking back more than a hundred years. Prison records are generally closed for a hundred years as well.

Workhouse records make for especially interesting reading as they often contain detailed physical descriptions of inmates. In fact, workhouse records are, unfortunately, often ports of call for those tracing their Victorian ancestry. And they are particularly useful sources of information between the years 1837–75. During this period, civil registration was in its infancy and events that should have been reported to the local registrar were not submitted; workhouses, however, kept their own registers of births, baptisms, deaths and burials.

It was the Poor Law Amendment Act of 1834 that cast the monstrous shadow of the workhouse over countless lives. The Act was supposedly designed for the benefit of those who couldn't support themselves: outdoor relief (usually grants of money from district relieving officers) was, for the most part, abolished and paupers were admitted to a workhouse instead. In practice, this meant 'out of sight, out of mind'.

Conditions in the workhouses were deliberately made as unpleasant as possible, to discourage the 'idle poor' from benefiting from the institutions. Anyone even remotely able-bodied would go to enormous lengths to avoid being admitted, and people would endure appalling cold and hunger before applying to the workhouse. There were several reasons for this, the first on the list being that husbands and wives were separated from each other and from their children. Further-more, everyone was required to eat in absolute silence and food was usually inadequate amounts of gruel, broth, potatoes and bread. Visitors were banned, except by special permission, and the ill, pregnant and insane were lodged, often indiscriminately, in tiny cots crammed together. Infants would be moved out to baby farms, establishments created to reduce the mortality rate amongst paupers. They would stay there until they were aged six, at which point they were apprenticed or returned to their local workhouse – if, that is, they survived the farm. Child mortality rates in rural areas were around sixty per cent. In towns they were as high as ninety per cent.

The Poor Law Amendment Act did not, in reality, make much difference to the lives of the poor. Four years after it was passed, the *London Journal* described the plight of the poor in the capital.

Imagine men, women, children, all barefooted, ploughing through the nasty, filthy mire. Some were leaning against the wall for lack of a place to sit, others were squatting on the ground, there were children lying about in the mud like pigs ... I saw children without a stitch of clothing, young girls, nursing mothers with no shoes on their feet, wearing only a tattered shift which barely covered their naked bodies ... Inside and out the decrepit hovels are like the rags of the people who live in them. Neither the windows nor the doors of most of these lodgings can be closed off; floors are mostly bare earth ... everyone sleeps in the one room, father, mother, sons, daughters and friends, like so many animals.

On the sliding scale of slums, those would not have been the worst. At the bottom of the barrel was Jacob's Island, a putrefying backwater in Bermondsey, almost exclusively inhabited by the criminal classes. Charles Knight, in *Passages of a Working Life*, his acclaimed exploration of Victorian London, wrote:

Whoever ventures here finds the streets, by courtesy so called, thronged with loiterers, and sees, through half-glazed windows, rooms crowded to suffocation. The stagnant gutters in the middle of the lanes, the filth choking up the dark passages which open up onto the highways, all these scarce leave so dispiriting an impression on the passenger as the condition of the houses. Walls the colour of bleached soot, doors falling from their hinges, door-posts worm-eaten, windows where shivered panes of glass alternate with wisps of straw, old hats and lumps of bed-ticken or brown paper, bespeak the last and frailest shelter that can be interposed between man and the elements.

Part of the point of places like Jacob's Island is that few people *did* dare to venture forth to them. They were, effectively, criminal communities. Even the police were wary of going anywhere near them. They were very much about 'looking after your own'. Thievery didn't generally take place within these communities: rather, thieves ventured from them to more affluent parts of the city to ply their trade. And these communities provided training grounds from an early age. Adults who had been transported, imprisoned or had gone elsewhere in search of work often left their children in one of the lodging houses that provided a front for professional child thieves. Some of them even ran schools for professional pickpockets in their kitchens. Independence, even for small children, was a highly valued commodity. And those children became adults very quickly. They had to: in the more desperate slums, the average age of death was seventeen. But they had time enough to become parents: the age of consent was twelve.

It is impossible to gauge how many people lived like that. It is also highly likely that, if you have an ancestor unfortunate enough to have lived in such conditions, you'll never find him or her. As Hilary Hale, an amateur genealogist researching her family in London, says, 'Unless you were very bad or very grand, it was so easy to just disappear from all records.' If you were very grand, you would appear in all the records, in newspapers and on your illustrious family tree. And if you were very bad, you would be recorded as a prison inmate.

The Act of 1823 made justices of the peace responsible for the upkeep of prisons, so there are records from that date on prison conditions, with lists of prisoners, their ages and the offences they committed. It also required prison governors to keep journals – hence the detailed information that exists today.

Most prison journals can be found in the prisons themselves, in county records offices or equivalent local borough archives. All criminal registers from 1805 are available for consultation at the PRO. There are myriad other records available there, especially those pertaining to prisons and jails in the London area, of which there were many.

Court Systems and Records

To make your research into prison records easier, it is essential to understand the various types of court system used in this country. While Britain is generally regarded as the greatest country in the world for genealogical information, the sheer volume of bureaucratic records this entails can also prove to be something of a headache for family researchers. Other countries' records have been damaged by earthquakes, hurricanes, termites, incessant wars, political upheaval (Communism, for example) or indeed bureaucratic inertia. But Britain has been keeping and maintaining records for the past thousand years, especially in the area of the administration of justice, both civil and criminal. It should also be remembered that a great deal of the early courts' business wasn't to do with civil liberties or criminal justice but with enforcing the power (and filling the exchequer) of the monarch.

There were, and still are, innumerable types of court in the United Kingdom. There are also a surprising number of records still in existence, even from some of the very earliest systems of justice. One system was known as the General Eyre, which operated from 1194–1294. It may have begun even earlier, but no records before that date survive. An Eyre involved sending out justices from the central courts at Westminster, to hold courts in all the counties of England, originally to try certain types of property litigation formulated during the reign of Henry II (1154–89). Soon, however, Eyre justices acquired a wider jurisdiction and they were hearing all the crown pleas from the county that had arisen since the last Eyre. And much of what they heard concerned the king's proprietary rights and offences against royal prerogatives and the conduct of local officials. The General Eyre was suspended in 1294 but there were occasional attempts to revive it in the fourteenth and the sixteenth centuries.

The surviving Eyre records, known as Eyre Rolls, can be found at the PRO. Most of them are fragmentary and are written almost entirely in Latin, often very much abbreviated. So, unless you have a knowledge of that language and its medieval legal applications, you're not likely to understand what you find. Realistically, you are highly unlikely to be looking back as far as the Eyre Rolls in the first place. You may, however, find records of trials in the manorial records kept in medieval times. Some criminals were tried at the Court Leet, a court presided over by the lord of the manor. But by the mid sixteenth century, lords of the manor no longer had jurisdiction over criminal law, and justices of the peace were appointed by the king instead.

You are far more likely to be looking for criminal ancestors in the records of the Assizes, a system of trial by itinerant judges that took place twice a year, from the thirteenth century until 1971, when the Assizes were replaced by crown courts. Early Assize records are patchy and only start to survive in quantity from 1559 onwards. Assizes generally dealt with serious crime, as petty crimes were usually heard in local courts at Quarter Sessions in front of justices of the peace every three months. If they were held in a town, the sessions were called Borough Sessions.

Ancient Assize records are often unreliable. Early ones don't give the age of the accused or details of family and, all too often, the accused would use an alias and lie about their occupation or where they lived. Furthermore, Assize records before 1733 are nearly all in Latin. If you don't know where or when the accused was tried, it is essential (until the nineteenth century) to know the county or circuit in which your ancestor was tried, as lists are not indexed by personal name but by circuit. From 1805, you can look at Criminal Registers (for England and Wales) which list people charged with indictable offences and give the place of trial, verdict and sentence.

As for the records themselves, you're likely to find, in the *Crown Minute Book*, the name of the accused, the case heard, the plea, the verdict and the sentence. Other miscellaneous information for some trials survives in the form of unwieldy bundles containing records such as jury panels and coroners inquests. Transcripts of court proceedings or shorthand notes of what was actually said in court do not normally survive. This is where newspaper reports of the trials really come into their own – and is where most of the information on the trials shown in *The People Detective* was gleaned.

The Assize courts did not cover all of England. Some counties were governed differently from others and, in the case of Cheshire, Durham and Lancashire, had their own courts along similar lines to the Assizes. These were known as 'Palatinate courts' and were abolished in the nineteenth century and subsequently included in Assize courts.

London, too, was different. Grouped with Middlesex, it generally saw petty crimes tried by the Lord Mayor and Aldermen of the city of London. Cases similar to those heard at the Assizes and cases deemed to be of national importance were heard at the Old Bailey. It became the most important criminal court in England and, after 1834, was officially known as the Central Criminal Court.

Prior to 1543, Wales was subject to its own laws. From that date until 1830, the Welsh equivalent of the Assizes was known as the Courts of Great Sessions. In 1830, the Assize system was extended to Wales.

Ireland's system of justice was much the same as that of England, although the country did have some of its own courts. The Courts Martial, for example, were established after the 1798 rebellion, to deal with insurrections. All records are stored in the National Archives, but another source – newspapers – can be even more enlightening than court records. Trials and cases heard in all courts were recorded in local newspapers.

Scottish law is different from English law and so is its administration. North of the border, Sheriff courts dealt (and still deal) with minor offences, and most records survive in the National Archives from about the late eighteenth century. They generally contain more information than their English equivalents. Justices of the peace also tried minor offences while the High Court of Judiciary, the highest criminal court in Scotland, sat in Edinburgh and on circuit.

Further Information

Witchcraft and Folklore
Folklore Society
Warburg Institute
Woburn Square
London WC1H 0AB
Tel: 020 7862 8264

Court Records
National Archives of Ireland
Bishop Street
Dublin 8
Tel: 00 3531 407 2300/2333
www.nationalarchives.ie

National Archives of Scotland
HM General Register House
Princes Street
Edinburgh EH1 3YY
Tel: 0131 535 1314
www.nas.gov.uk

Public Record Office (PRO)
Ruskin Avenue
Kew
Surrey TW9 4DU
Tel: 020 8392 5200
www.pro.gov.uk

JAMES CHALMERS,
the Victorian Missionary

The British Abroad: Tracing Emigrants
✤
Child Migration Schemes

On Easter Monday 1901, James Chalmers stepped ashore on Goaribari Island, off the southern coast of Papua New Guinea, intent on converting the islanders to Christianity. The Goaribari, however, had other ideas. They clubbed him unconscious, decapitated him, cut him into small pieces, boiled him with sago and ate him.

'"Served him right," was what my grandmother used to say,' recalls Charlotte Sainsbury, a descendant of Chalmers' wife, Jane Hercus. 'The family line on him was that he was a dour, Scottish Presbyterian, interfering sort of figure. Very Cromwellian: whipping everyone into shape and never enjoying himself.'

It's not entirely surprising that the family held this view of Chalmers. Both literature and legend are full of tales of Victorian muscular Christians bludgeoning savages with the Bible and destroying their indigenous way of life. The truth, however, was often more complex and, in the case of James Chalmers, entirely different. But all Charlotte knew about him when she wrote to *The People Detective* was her grandmother's theory, corroborated by a scribble on the family tree reading, 'Missionary, eaten by cannibals.' (Incidentally, Charlotte's family tree was researched by previous generations who traced the family back to James V of Scotland.)

Charlotte soon learnt, through the investigations of *The People Detective*, that James Chalmers had fortunately been an enlightened missionary. He was born in 1841 in Argyllshire, Scotland, and, by his own account, was always 'very restless and dearly loved adventure, and a dangerous position was exhilarating'. Aged eighteen, he applied to the London Missionary Society and was sent by them to Cheshunt College for theological training, where he was noted by a fellow student as: 'active and muscular ... a born pioneer and leader of men'.

In 1865, he married one Jane Hercus, and in January of the next year they sailed to Australia *en route* to their first mission on the island of Rarotonga, where they remained until 1877, when Chalmers received instructions to move on to New Guinea – an island largely unexplored at the time. 'Several bands of native teachers from the islands,' he later wrote, 'went to New Guinea during that period, but only a few survived the ferocity of the cannibals and the trying climatic conditions.'

Chalmers, of course, relished the challenge and, although there was a tense stand-off period when he arrived (during which one native was killed), he was accepted and trusted, partly due to the fact that he brought goods with him.

Chalmers was the absolute antithesis of the old-school fire-and-brimstone preacher. Traditionally, missionaries barely recognised indigenous cultures and beliefs. Chalmers, however, believed in living among the communities and using games and fun in the classroom to preach the gospel. And it is believed that in order to win the trust of one tribe he participated in the *Moguru* ritual; little more than a homosexual orgy. He was certainly a hard-drinking, fun-loving, flamboyant soul who incurred the displeasure and often the wrath of other missionaries. His autobiography reveals his hostile attitudes to some of his fellow missionaries, who resented his stubborn determination to pursue his own pioneering agenda. And it was that agenda which lead to his death. For, after the retirement of James MacFarlane, the austere Presbyterian head of the mission in the west of New Guinea, he deceived the other missionaries into believing that he had the permission of the London Missionary Society to expand his mission westwards.

Towards the end of his life, his letters – and those of fellow missionary Oliver Tomkins, who was killed with him on Goaribari – attest to depression which, combined with his single-mindedness, may account for that fatal trip. The manner of his death led to punitive expeditions by the British and subsequently, in 1904, the expedition to recover the remains of Chalmers.

The saga of James Chalmers is extremely well documented. His murder – and that of his young colleague – made headlines all over the world and his letters and diaries are found today in the Missionary Society archives at the School of Oriental and African Studies (SOAS) in London. Books have been published about him and the manuscript for his own autobiography was found in Papua New Guinea after his death. Yet a century down the line, he has largely been forgotten. The popular conception of missionaries probably hasn't helped; it is likely that others shared his descendants' attitude that if he didn't want to be eaten, he shouldn't have gone there in the first place. And it probably doesn't help that Papua New Guinea is but a pinprick on the world's consciousness.

So, Charlotte Sainsbury had absolutely no idea that, by following the footsteps of her ancestor, she would become both a national heroine and a threat, be discussed in print and would cause a diplomatic rumpus. 'I suppose I thought if the story proved interesting, it might make a minute of television,' she recalls with a wry grin. 'I had absolutely no conception of where it might lead.'

James Chalmers is now revered in Papua New Guinea. 'Practically every second word is "Chalmers",' says Charlotte. She also noticed that, if the islanders weren't invoking Chalmers, they were invoking Christ: 'They're an incredibly religious people and, to be honest, when we went there I felt something of a fraud. I think they expected me to be like my ancestor.'

So what was James Chalmers really like? 'It appears he was exactly the opposite of what I had envisaged; a bit of a hell-raiser, I think. If they ever make a film about him, then Billy Connolly should play the part – judging by the photos, he's a dead ringer, and just like him in temperament as well.' Furthermore, he was one of those missionaries who believed in doing the right thing by the people he was amongst and he, more than anyone, succeeded in disengaging a clannish society from perpetual warfare – and stopped them from eating their enemies. 'They said he took Christianity to them in a way that really helped,' recalls Charlotte. 'Apparently he wanted them to keep some of their own customs, such as not wearing clothes – very unusual for a missionary in those times. And he wanted them to keep their art. From what they said to me, they really appreciated that.'

If it seems odd that, after more than a century, James Chalmers features so prominently in the national consciousness, it's because of the demographics and culture of that nation. Simon Everson, who directed the *People Detective* episode in Papua New Guinea, says: 'The villages are essentially the same as they were fifty or a hundred years ago. They're very isolated and there aren't many roads. We had to go everywhere by plane – and everywhere we went the entire village turned out to see us. It's not an integrated society; very clannish.' Given the lack of infrastructure and integration, it's not surprising that traditions and tales are handed down from generation to generation by word of mouth. And the story of James Chalmers, to the astonishment of the *People Detective* team, was on everyone's lips. Part of the reason why his story is so fresh appears to be because of his extraordinary charisma. The other reason is that his death is a huge embarrassment to the people of Papua New Guinea.

This is where the plot thickened and embroiled the *People Detective* crew in a parliamentary debate. 'They adore him,' says Charlotte. 'Basically, he stopped them eating each other – only to be eaten himself.' Chalmers' death, and its repercussions, still rankle with the Papua New Guineans. The subject is fraught, lengthy and complex, but the basics are that Chalmers ventured to the island of Goaribari against the wishes of the London Missionary Society and, more pertinently, completely unannounced. Charlotte gave her explanation of the islanders' behaviour: 'They were only doing what they had been doing for centuries. I think it was a fairly bloody sort of life out there, and if someone came along who they didn't know he would be assumed to be the enemy and would be killed and eaten.'

The repercussions, however, were devastating – and on two counts. Firstly, the British and, subsequently, the Australians (under whose authority the country was placed in 1902) sent people in to burn down villages in a seemingly indiscriminate fashion and, secondly, the Goaribari islanders were ostracised by the rest of the country. 'I was in a really strange position,' recalls Charlotte, 'there were so many different levels. On the one hand I was being treated like royalty and on the other, I felt guilty at being somehow responsible for what had happened. More than anything else, I wanted to help the tribe that had been ostracised.'

That is why the presence of the TV crew nearly caused a diplomatic incident. The governor of the Gulf Province (in which Goaribari is situated) requested, in Parliament, that the crew be ordered out because, as the governor claimed, 'they had not notified provincial authorities about the project.' He went on to say that the villagers of Goaribari still harboured resentment over civil authority (the country only achieved self-government in 1973 and independence in 1975) and would resent outsiders trying to revive a past that they would rather forget. The government minister to whom this plea was addressed replied that the crew had been allowed into the country and could proceed to the Gulf Province because they had fulfilled the necessary formalities required by the National Cultural Commission and the Foreign Affairs Department.

All of this demonstrates that bureaucracy cannot be easily implemented in a country that has traditionally operated through its own particular brand of democracy. 'The thing is,' says Simon Everson, 'society operates in a completely different way. Although we had the requisite permits, we really needed to approach absolutely everybody who might be involved. If we wanted to film in a particular place, it didn't matter that we had official permission. What we needed, unofficially, was permission from the community; from the people who owned the land. It was quite obvious that society operated in that way: in every village we went to the inhabitants would gather beneath the stilts of a house in the centre, debate issues and nominate a spokesman to confer with us.'

The *People Detective* team were accompanied by a Papua New Guinean anthropologist who knew the culture (if not all the languages spoken in the country), yet they never did get to the village where Chalmers was murdered. They did, however, meet several of the descendants of the tribesmen who had killed and supposedly eaten James Chalmers. 'Some of the people from that village,' recalls Simon Everson, 'had moved to Port Moresby, the capital, and we got into a sort of powwow with them. It was fascinating, mainly because we were trying to tell the story as much from their perspective as from ours. Their view was that they had to live with the terrible shame of having been responsible for Chalmers' death and that they didn't want to go further down that route.'

A curious aspect of the talks is that both Charlotte and Simon got the impression that the tribe responsible still possessed artefacts of Chalmers'. Or indeed parts of Chalmers himself. 'They told me they had something of Chalmers' that they would return to me at some point,' says Charlotte. 'But I'm not sure if I want it. Supposing it's his skull?' 'I can understand why they didn't spill the beans,' is Simon's reaction. 'They didn't want us to exploit them and get nothing in return. And in a way it was better like that because we got into long talks with them and established some sort of rapport. But my gut feeling is that they have something of Chalmers'. Whether it's his skull or a possession, I don't know.'

A little ghoulish, perhaps, but believable. Charlotte Sainsbury was informed that the reprisals by the British and the Australians were partly due to the islanders' reluctance for some reason, to return James Chalmers' skull for burial. Several skulls were, apparently, submitted before the one that was deemed to be his was accepted. Yet his burial place, which was visited by the crew, is nowadays revered and, to this day, tended by the people of Papua New Guinea.

The visit to Papua New Guinea by *The People Detective* mirrored in some ways Chalmers' own visit. 'When we got there,' recalls Charlotte, 'we took a boat to the first village he ever visited. The sea was really rough and there we were, rocking around like nothing on earth for ten hours. But the slightly eerie thing was looking at the coastline: there's forest right the way down to the water and you don't see a single sign of life, yet somehow you know there are people watching you all the way along. And, arriving at each village, we had absolutely no idea how we were going to be treated.'

The team were, without exception, treated like visiting dignitaries. 'In one village, it was almost as if I were a queen. They were actually very distressed we hadn't warned them we were coming, because they would have carried us through the village on a litter. And, when the whole village had gathered round us, I was put on a stage and expected to give a speech – something I've never done in my life! It was completely overwhelming.'

'I filmed all those meetings,' says Simon, 'and they really

must have been very similar to Chalmers' own experiences. Everyone gathered beneath one of the huts on stilts, discussing the situation with the head man who would then approach us. Even if the anthropologist with us didn't understand the language he would know when to nudge Charlotte and tell her that she was expected to say something.'

Charlotte obviously said the right things and her royal tour progressed. But one of the things she wanted to know was if cannibalism still existed, and she asked several people if it did. 'I met a lot of Papua New Guineans and, yes, I did ask if there were still any remote tribes involved in cannibalism. Everyone denied it. I think, unsurprisingly, they're quite embarrassed about it. But you know, there are still tribes that have never seen any white men and who live in incredibly remote regions ...'

'I asked as well,' says Simon, 'and heard rumours that it still happened as recently as twenty years ago. I also asked about the reasons for it. You know, was it a spiritual thing, or was it all about picking up your enemy's strength? Apparently it was much more simple: it was about anger. If you were really angry with your enemy you ate him.'

'But,' continues Simon, 'they do have really strange, slightly cannibalistic ways of dealing with their dead. They put them in a sort of cradle off the ground and leave the body to decompose. It's actually completely disgusting: the body fats and fluids run into a bowl underneath. Then they have a sort of feast and dip their food into the bowl. I think it's called "endo-cannibalism". And I was told there are instances of a disease of the nervous system – like mad cow disease – that could be to do with that funeral rite.'

Just a few years ago there was another, even closer, parallel to

James Chalmers' experiences, which also took place in Papua New Guinea. The writer Edward Marriott set out to track down the Liawep, a 'lost tribe' reported to have been discovered living a Stone-Age existence in the mountainous rainforest. Refused official permission to visit the area, he nevertheless persisted, only to discover after six days of trekking through unmapped jungle that the tribe had fled in fear of his approach and that virtually the only person left was a mentally deranged Lutheran missionary called Herod.

In his book about his adventure, Marriott describes how he managed to win the confidence of several of the Liawep (although the majority remained hostile) and was even entrusted with the care of the wife and baby of one of the tribesmen during a hunting trip. Then disaster struck: during a massive tropical storm, his charges and three other children were killed by lightning. Marriott was told, in no uncertain terms, that he must flee or be murdered and so, miserable, frightened, guilty and confused, and well aware that he was reneging on his responsibilities to his friend, he realised he had to run.

There followed a headlong chase through the jungle, with the Liawep in hot pursuit. This last part of the book is one of the most compelling, harrowing and poignant pieces of prose you will ever find in a book of travels. Marriott finally managed to evade the Liawep and, unlike the hapless James Chalmers, escaped with his life.

Marriott's take on the missionaries in 1990s Papua New Guinea is almost as interesting as his encounter with the Liawep. His version is that they are cast in an entirely different mould from James Chalmers and that they are using crude

One of Mary Bateman's most audacious ploys was apparently to claim her hen laid eggs bearing the inscription 'Christ is Come.' In fact, Mary wrote the inscription herself and then reinserted the eggs into the unfortunate hen before inviting people to watch the 'miracle' that ensued.

A drawing of Mary Bateman and two of her hapless victims, the Perigos. They were the most gullible of her targets; she fleeced them of everything they possessed and Rebecca Perigo died after taking Mary's 'remedy'.

MARY BATEMAN.

The Yorkshire Witch.

Left: Public dissection was a great spectator sport in the eighteenth and early nineteenth centuries. People paid to see the corpses of criminals such as Mary Bateman publicly dissected in the name of medical research.

Below left: The skull of Mary Bateman, the Yorkshire witch. Both it and her skeleton are on display at the Thackray Medical Museum, Leeds.

Right: Although he appears the epitome of the dour Presbyterian missionary, James Chalmers was a hard-drinking, fun-loving and highly adventurous individual.

Below: James Chalmers stayed in this house on stilts in Papua New Guinea. He was killed and eaten by cannibals on Easter Monday, 1901.

Above: Artist Claughton Pellew was incarcerated in Dartmoor Prison during World War One for being a conscientious objector. He never fully recovered from his harsh treatment there.

Below: Claughton Pellew's great-niece, Sarah Apps, relives her ancestor's days in prison. A chilling experience.

This map shows the fifteen hundred acres of parish granted to the infamous Maroons of Jamaica in 1739.

Spencer Fearon is shown how his ancestors would use leaves to camouflage themselves in the Jamaican forests.

An inscription on the gravestone of one of Spencer's ancestors. The graveyard is in the garden of his Jamaican relations' home.

Left: 'Gloria' – real name May Kenworthy – was the face of the 1930s and the original supermodel. She was photographed tens of thousands of time in her career.

Right: The original advertisement for Ovaltine. The likeness is popularly believed to be that of Gloria.

Below: The camera never lies, it just tampers with the truth ... Gloria's descendant Clare Cowley models 1930s fashions.

Above: Daru Rooke searches for court records of the Florence Maybrick trial in Liverpool Library.

Below: A court artist's drawing of Florence Maybrick on trial for the murder of her husband in Liverpool in 1889 – one of the most sensational trials of the time.

bribery (vague promises of wealth, education and hospitals) as well as threats (of damnation) to forcibly uproot all that is left of the indigenous culture.

The *People Detective* trip revealed that much of this culture still exists – but that it is indeed changing. 'It's awful in a way,' says Charlotte Sainsbury, 'because you know the world will change them. They're still living in straw huts and making boats out of canoes, but it won't last.' Indeed Charlotte had first-hand proof of that: 'When I said I was leaving, one man in a remote village said we could keep in touch by e-mail. I was stunned. Anyway, we can't: *I* don't have e-mail!'

From James Chalmers' Autobiography, Life and Work in New Guinea, 1895.

I asked him [a native] why they ate human flesh. He told me that it was the women of the tribes who first urged the men to kill their fellow human beings for the purpose of eating them. The husbands were, the man told me, returning from a successful hunt far inland. As was their custom, they were blowing their conch-shells and singing and dancing.

As they approached the village, coming down the river in their canoes piled high with wallabies, boars and cassowaries, the women called out to them: 'What success, husbands, that you sing and dance so?' 'Great success,' the men shouted back. 'Plenty to eat. Here, come and see for yourselves.'

The women approached the canoes, and when they saw what was in them, they called out: 'What, just that dirty stuff?' And then, in voices of scorn: 'Who is going to eat that? Is that what you call successful hunting?'

Then the men began reasoning among themselves: 'What do our wives mean, mocking us like this?' And one of them, wiser than the others, said after much thought: 'I know. They want the flesh of man!'

Then, throwing the wallabies and boars and cassowaries over the sides of their canoes, they went quickly along the river to a neighbouring village and brought back with them ten bodies. But, the man said to me, the men returned in their canoes without their usual singing and rejoicing.

When the women who were waiting for them on the riverbank saw them approaching the village, they called out: 'What have our husbands brought for us to eat, this time?' And then they looked, but their husbands did not look at them, only cast their eyes downwards at what lay in their canoes. 'Yes, that is right!' shouted the women. 'Dance and sing again, now, for you have brought back with you something worth dancing and singing about!'

Then the ten bodies were taken out of the canoes and put on the riverbank. And the women cooked them, and pronounced them good. And from that day till now, the men and women of these tribes have always said that the flesh of human beings is better than the flesh of any other animal.

The British Abroad: Tracing Emigrants

Because James Chalmers was a missionary and frequently reported back to the London Missionary Society, his life abroad was extremely well documented (his sensational fate helped a bit, too). The records of most missionary societies can be consulted directly, and many other societies have donated archives to SOAS. To use their library, you may need a letter of recommendation from the missionary society concerned.

Descendants of other Britons who lived abroad may not have such a large amount of information available to them, but there are, nonetheless, many sources for consultation. This is partly due to the worldwide nature of genealogy. If family history is something of a passion in Great Britain, it's near obsession in some countries, particularly the United States. Countless people there are researching their family trees, trying and often succeeding in finding links back to Britain. Hundreds of thousands of Britons left for America in the seventeenth and eighteenth centuries and, in the nineteenth century, emigration reached tidal-wave proportions with around ten million people leaving for America and parts of the Empire. Today, with millions of people researching their family trees, it's likely (especially if you have internet access) that you'll encounter other people investigating emigration and, probably, the same family as you yourself are researching.

People emigrated for many reasons; some of the earliest emigrants were fleeing religious persecution. The Edict of Expulsion of 1290, for example, decreed that all Jews in England were to be baptised, banished or put to death. Nearly four hundred years of intolerance followed until, in 1656, Oliver Cromwell revoked the Edict, and Jews were permitted to enter the country freely. Similarly, Catholics in England had a particularly hard time when the Protestant Elizabeth I assumed the throne, following the reign of her fanatically Catholic half-sister Mary. The Act of Supremacy and Uniformity was passed in 1559, which made it illegal for a Catholic mass to be celebrated in England and Wales. This state of affairs continued until 1778, when the Catholic Relief Act was passed.

Another reason why many people left these shores, from the seventeenth century onwards, was because they were convicted criminals and were transported. Yet probably the main reason for Britons emigrating was a time-honoured and still relevant economic one: hundreds of thousands of people went in search of a better life. Thousands of this number were assisted in their emigration, with many working as indentured servants in the colonies, especially in America and the West Indies. They would generally agree to work, usually on plantations, for a certain number of years in exchange for payment for their passage and board and, after completing their term of service, a grant of freehold land and some cash. Forms of assisted emigration continued until well into the twentieth century, when people were encouraged to move to Australia and New Zealand: their passage would cost the princely sum of ten pounds – hence the expression 'ten pound poms'.

So where do you start looking for ancestors who left the country? Fortunately, there are numerous sources, including published guides to records for the country of emigration, and numerous documents at the PRO. There are many references to individuals and families emigrating at the PRO, but no single index to the names of such persons. The chief sources of information held there are the Colonial Office records and those of the Home Office, Board of Trade and Treasury.

Many overseas libraries and record offices have copies of original material, notably the Library of Congress in Washington, the Public Archives of Canada in Ottawa, the National Library at Canberra and the Mitchell Library in

Sydney. A very good route to adopt is to join one of the Family History Societies in the country you are interested in. To do this, contact the Federation of Family History Societies or the Society of Genealogists. The latter also has what is probably the best collection of printed material, and this can be consulted for a small fee. So, too, the Mormon church is a brilliant source of information for people who emigrated from Britain. As the Mormons have a remit to locate all their ancestors, in order to baptise them into their church, a vast number of names have been traced back to the British Isles. Again, it must be emphasised that information compiled by the Mormon church (and indeed by any other organisation) should be checked against original documents. *The British Overseas* (Geoffrey Yeo, 1984) is published by the Guildhall Library and is also a good source for research.

The purpose of *The People Detective* was not just to locate ancestors and descendants, but also to recreate what life was like for them. In this respect, researching ancestors abroad can be especially rewarding and exciting. It is, for example, a common American dream to find that you are descended from the earliest settlers in North America: the Puritans who sailed on the *Mayflower*. The Puritans were never a specific Nonconformist denomination; it was a general term for those, especially in Elizabethan and Stuart times, who wished to carry the reformation of the Church of England further by purifying it of all ceremony. Some thought they could best do this away from England, and set off on the *Mayflower*.

It is, however, completely untrue that the passengers on the *Mayflower* were the first to colonise that continent. The *Mayflower* arrived in New England in 1620, yet emigration from

Britain to the Americas began in 1585 when Sir Walter Ralegh founded a settlement off the coast of North Carolina. True, it failed, but a settlement of 1607 in Jamestown, Virginia, succeeded and became the centre of a thriving colony. So it is something of an urban Bostonian myth that the 'true blue' settlers became New Englanders; Virginia, really, is where it all began. Myths, however, are incredibly difficult to shift; anyone who has been to New England will know that the puritan spirit lives on, but modern New Englanders may be interested to know that a minority (thirty-six people) of the *Mayflower*'s passengers were Puritan refugees.

Although British emigrants travelled almost everywhere in the world, America has always been the favoured destination. It's estimated that, from 1630–1700, more than half a million people left Britain and that about four hundred thousand of them went to America. Jump forward to the nineteenth century and you'll find that nearly ten million people left these shores. This increase came about with the advent of the railways, which meant easy access to ports, although famine in Ireland also contributed to the huge exodus.

The most obvious and the easiest way of discovering when and where your ancestors left England is to look at ships' passenger lists but, unfortunately, records of these at the PRO only date back to 1890 and the way they have been compiled means that you need to know either the name of the ship on which your ancestor sailed or the approximate date of sailing. However, because of the sheer volume of emigrants from these shores, colossal amounts of research have been undertaken by individuals and non-governmental organisations. One such organisation, the Immigrant Ships Transcribers Guild, has done an amazing job in locating lists from all over the world. Their web site, located at: (no www) istg.rootsweb.com/index1.htm, is superb and, at the time of writing, has around twenty-eight thousand lists for consultation. There are some forty lists for Glasgow, and even an 1848 listing for the island of South Uist, in Scotland. Furthermore, the database is searchable by surname and is definitely worth a try.

Apart from ships' lists, there are countless other sources available to the family researcher. The PRO holds Privy Council Registers spanning the years 1540–1978, which contain numerous entries about the colonies. It also holds records relating to individual colonies. There are also Plantation Books from 1678–1806 and Treasury Board Papers from 1557–1920, containing many references to people entering or exiting the colonies. There is a welter of other information from sources such as Chancery Patent Rolls (pertaining to the granting of offices and lands) and Passport Registers from as far back as 1795 (passports were not legally required until 1914 so, usually, only diplomats or merchants applied for one). The records available at the PRO are too vast to itemise here, but you should consider visiting it yourself, or consulting the myriad publications listed there and at the many large university and public libraries that concern themselves with emigration.

Child Migration Schemes

Some of the most poignant stories of emigration concern the transportation of poor children or orphans to Australia, Canada, New Zealand and other parts of the Empire. This happened mainly in the latter part of the nineteenth century and continued well into the twentieth. Child migration schemes originated in 1617, when the Virginia Company in America asked for children to be sent to boost the numbers of their fledgling colony and the City of London sent more than one hundred children from Christ's Hospital School. (Records from that school, established in 1553 to provide free schooling for children of freemen of the City of London, are held at the Guildhall library.)

Latterly, in the late nineteenth and twentieth centuries, one of the biggest child migration schemes was the 'Home Children' scheme. This was an exercise in populating the Commonwealth with 'good white British stock' and is today one of the most popular areas of genealogical enquiry. Thousands of people – particularly on the internet – make enquiries about the origins of their parents or grandparents who arrived in far-flung areas of the Commonwealth with nothing more than a name to identify them. This is particularly interesting, given that it is such a relatively recent phenomenon and, in many ways, such a barbaric one.

From 1882–1908, Dr Barnardo shipped fourteen per cent (4500) of his children to Canada illegally, i.e. without parental consent. A further 3000 were sent because of court orders and the Home Secretary's authorisation. And Barnardo's was not the only organisation to ship children abroad: fifty British child-care institutions sent 73,000 children to Canada alone, all of them unaccompanied by parents or guardians. Few of the children from the institutions had ever travelled more than a few miles from their place of birth and had absolutely no idea of what was involved in being transported to a different continent.

The government and children's homes didn't seem to care much either. Children shipped to Canada, for example (boys in the spring and girls in the autumn), were issued with a suitcase or trunk containing: a cap, a suit, a belt, a ball of wool, a boot brush, one pair of rubber boots, one pair of slippers, one pair of overalls, one set of underwear, two long night-shirts, two pairs of woollen socks, two shirts, two handkerchiefs, some needles and some thread. Each case also contained a copy of the Bible.

In 1924, an enquiry, the Bondfield Commission, concluded that British children sent to Canada suffered from loss of education, overwork and non-payment for their labour on farms. The Commission recommended that children should be given long winter trousers to replace their short ones and that children under the age of fourteen should not be sent abroad to work. This held true for the other most popular destinations for children – Australia and Rhodesia (now Zimbabwe).

Further Information

Missionary Records
Church Mission Society
The Archivist
Partnership House
157 Waterloo Road
London SE1 8UU
Tel: 020 7928 8681

School of African and Oriental Studies (SOAS)
Library Archives
Thornhaugh Street
Russell Square
London WC1H OXG
Tel: 020 7898 4180

Home Children
Barnardo's Head Office
Tanners Lane
Barkingside
Ilford
Essex IG6 1QG
Tel: 020 8550 8822
www.barnardos.org.uk

CLAUGHTON PELLEW,
the Conscientious Objector

Conscientious Objectors
✦
Military Records
✦
Naval Records

When *The People Detective* researched Claughton Pellew's story for the series, many sources of genealogical research had to be investigated. Claughton's story led the programme researchers deep into the records of institutions ranging from the Tate Gallery Archive and Imperial War Museum, to the PRO and Peace Pledge Union.

Yet Claughton Pellew's story would never have seen the light of day but for David Gore and his personal interest in family history. David is the father of Sarah Apps (Claughton's great-niece), who featured in the television episode. His interest in genealogy was, initially, sparked by the fact that the Pellew family originated in Cornwall, where families, as David explains, 'kept themselves very much to themselves'. This came to an end when the staples of that county's economy, copper and tin, ran out, heralding the 'Great Emigration' that reached its peak towards the end of the nineteenth century. Described by historian A. L. Rowse as: 'the most significant event in the saga of the Cornish people', the emigration saw many mining families exporting their skills and traditions to the mines of North and South America, South Africa and Australia, where many of their descendants still live today.

Interest in both the ancient lineage of his Cornish forebears and their exodus from Cornwall led David Gore to research his family history, and to corroborate several family legends, one of which involved a connection to Edward VII's mistress, Lillie Langtry. 'One of her family went to Cornwall and married into our family: it was several generations further back than I envisaged but, really, there was a lot of luck involved because hers was a prominent Jersey family and very well documented. Normally, proving history is very difficult. In fifteen to twenty years of research into the family, I've come across pretty well all eventualities – and I've had to do a lot of guessing.'

Yet sometimes guesswork pays off. One of David's tips is that, when seemingly up against a dead end in family research, look at the careers your family favours. 'If you lose someone when families divide and go off to different countries, it's often worthwhile looking at their professions. A branch of my family, for example, went off to Australia and, like the branch that stayed in the UK, they became doctors. So doctors' records proved invaluable. Even if the two branches lose touch, it's not uncommon for them to be following the same career paths. That happens a lot in genealogy.'

With many years of experience as an amateur genealogist, David had several stories of interest to the *People Detective* team. Yet, as ever, proof of the actual blood tie was paramount; as was the 'interest factor' of the ancestor in question. Claughton Pellew proved to be a very interesting character indeed. Born in 1890, the great-grandson of Samuel Harvey and Philippa Pellew, both from ancient Cornish families, Claughton was taken to British Columbia by his parents, spent his early childhood in Canada and then, aged eleven, was taken back to Britain, where his father set up a thriving mining consultancy. Expected to follow in his family's footsteps as a mining engineer, Claughton disappointed his father by leaving home to study art. Four years at the Slade was followed by a trip to Italy which so influenced him that, in 1914, he converted to Catholicism.

Claughton became an artist of some considerable talent, who received many accolades from his peers – indeed he greatly influenced the painter John Nash. He looked set to become a renowned painter of pastoral scenes, but this never happened. Instead, he lived his adult life in obscurity and remained comparatively unknown as an artist. This may have been because of his stance on the First World War: he was a conscientious objector. Imprisoned during the war (unlike better-connected Bloomsbury Group pacifists like Mark Gertler and Duncan Grant), he never really recovered from the harsh treatment he received.

In October 1919, Claughton married another artist, Emma ('Kechie') Tennent, in Arundel, Sussex, who had also been a student at the Slade. Claughton and Kechie had no children of their own, but adopted Kechie's niece, Anne, when she was orphaned.

Although they travelled abroad on a regular basis, the Pellews became increasingly reclusive in England and, in 1926, they designed and built a house in a truly rural setting in Norfolk. There they remained, painting and entertaining a few loyal friends, for the rest of their lives. Kechie's health began to deteriorate in the 1950s and, at the expense of his own uncertain health, Claughton cared for her until he died in 1966. Two years later, Kechie died in a nursing home.

Despite his considerable talent as an artist and his connections with the art world, Claughton's work never became well known. One reason for Claughton's obscurity was his seeming lack of drive and ambition: his productive years ended in the 1930s, when the rural themes that formed the basis of his work were already out of fashion. His contemporary, John Nash, believed his lack of fame was principally to do with a sense of isolation, both spiritual and artistic. He felt that Claughton had been badly affected psychologically by his time in prison and that, after the war, he became largely alienated from society.

Vicky Greenly, Assistant Producer on *The People Detective*, who researched the Claughton story, made a surprising find relatively early on. In the Tate Gallery Archives, she stumbled across personal correspondence between Claughton and the Nash family. 'It was a complete surprise to me,' she explains. 'I had no idea there was an archive of Claughton's correspondence there. I went there to get a clearer picture of the Slade artists of the period and, instead, discovered through the letters that Claughton had an intense relationship with Christine Nash, John's wife.' This information contradicted the idea of the rural idyll that was supposedly led by Claughton and Kechie. It is also an example of how, by researching someone's background, unexpected material can emerge from unlikely sources. The Tate Archives, in fact, are a treasure house of information on artists, and contain some of their diaries, letters and personal memorabilia.

Conscientious Objectors

Various institutions hold records on conscientious objectors, or 'conchies', as they were called then. The term itself was coined during the First World War, yet the phenomenon of opposition to war on grounds of morality or faith was far from new: there are records of 'conscientious' objectors to the Napoleonic Wars and history is littered with accounts of pacifist opposition to war. Yet the First World War is unique in the history of British wars: it marked the introduction of compulsory military service in the country.

'I went to the Imperial War Museum,' recalls Vicky Greenly, 'where I knew there were records of conscientious objectors. I expected them to be rather formal and was surprised that there was a lot of personal and sometimes rather horrific information. I found one scrapbook that was really rather distressing. Someone had put together a lot of articles about what the military authorities used to do to conscientious objectors and it was horrific. They used to bang their heads against walls and beat them up and generally treat them like vermin.'

When the war began in 1914, the rush of volunteers was enormous. The nationwide surge of patriotism saw men flocking to the trenches and, at home, the anti-German feeling extended as far as people killing dachshunds in the streets. All this, however, changed when the sustained carnage in the trenches became general knowledge. And it didn't take long to filter through. 'Apparently,' says Vicky, 'people could hear the sound of gunfire from the Battle of the Somme over here in Britain.' That, along with the hundreds of thousands of lives lost and the tales of disease and hardship saw a marked change in the attitude to the war. Parliament, too, was obliged to change its policy. No longer able to rely on volunteers through vigorous recruitment campaigns, it passed the Military Service Act in 1916, introducing compulsory military service.

The Act allowed for applications to be made for exemption from the call-up on grounds of occupation, hardship, faith or moral belief, and a system of Military Service tribunals was set up to assess each application. In theory, this meant that those who saw the taking of life as wrong – amongst them Jehovah's Witnesses, Quakers and other Christian denominations – would be exempt from service. In practice, and from the surviving documents, the distinction between 'shirkers' and genuine cases was blurred and all applicants for exemption were distrusted.

In March 1916, Claughton Pellew was called before the local tribunal held at Greenwich and gave his occupation as an artist and, on the grounds of his conscientious objection, was given an exemption from combatant duties. That didn't mean an exemption from duty altogether: he was called up for non-combative service (activities like driving ambulances), but refused to go, instead turning himself in at Oxford police station. Sent to the magistrate's court for a hearing, he then spent a few days in the court cells, afterwards being sent to serve (non-combatant) in the Dorsetshire Regiment. However, he refused to have anything at all to do with the war and resisted all physical attempts to force him into uniform. The punishment for this was a court martial and, in Claughton's case, a sentence of 112 days in military detention barracks, where the harsh regime included a diet of bread and water.

He was subsequently transferred to a number of work camps under the Home Office Scheme, under which men were supposedly to undertake 'work of national importance'. In reality, this meant carrying out trivial tasks such as stone-breaking, sewing mail bags and making mats. His last incarceration was in Dartmoor Prison, where he spent twenty months working as a cook before being released, in the last few months of the war, for work on a Buckinghamshire farm.

Yet Claughton Pellew's ordeal did not end with the cessation of hostilities. Twenty years later, at the outbreak of World War Two, he was arrested as a suspected spy on the grounds that he was known to have German friends and could speak the language. He was held until his blameless British status could be established.

Some 16,000 conscientious objectors were, through Military Service tribunals, exempted from service in the First World War. Of those, the majority took up non-combatant duties or worked in work camps under the Home Office Scheme. Those who failed to convince the tribunals that they were anything other than 'shirkers' were sent to fight in France, where forty-one were sentenced to death for refusing to accept military discipline. Those who returned from France joined a total of 1298 conscientious objectors imprisoned for their views. Some of these men – the real 'absolutists' – spent as long as ten years in prison. Of their number, a further seventy died in prison: several had gone insane and committed suicide.

Despite the numbers involved and the procedures followed by

the military in assessing objections, it is notoriously difficult to find detailed information on conscientious objectors. This is principally because, in 1921, the Ministry of Health decided that all papers relating to individual cases of exemption from National Service should be destroyed. The vast majority of files from tribunals at which conchies were assessed were also destroyed. The reasons for the obliteration of these records remain unclear, but it has been assumed that either the government decided that conscientious objectors were simply too unimportant to rate historical mention, or that they were not thought worthy of recording, by dint of their shameful opposition to the national interest. Whatever the reason, the government succeeded in relegating the vast majority of records to the dustbin of history.

Some records, however, were kept as samples and others were not destroyed but may now be found in local Record Offices. Surviving records held at the PRO are few and far between. There were, however, other fascinating sources of information on conchies: information that, as is often the way with research, leads into new and fascinating areas. Research by *The People Detective* into the Claughton Pellew story revealed a wealth of information about both pacifism in general and the close connection between artists and peace movements. The Society of Friends, for example, first adopted their peace testimony in the 1660s, laying the foundations for Quaker pacifism. The Peace Pledge Union (PPU) was founded in 1934 and quickly became one of the most important organisations within the British peace movement. Its archives (accessed by appointment only) contain a wealth of information about conscientious objectors. It merged in 1937 with the No More War Movement (founded in 1921) and, together, their files include many prominent individuals. Amongst them are Vera Brittain, Aldous Huxley, Bertrand Russell, Siegfreid Sassoon, Benjamin Britten and Michael Tippett.

Research into conscientious objectors therefore leads, perhaps surprisingly, to a wealth of information on the intellectual life of a nation – and to its political life. The PPU at its peak was the world's largest absolute pacifist society and campaigned against conflicts including: the Spanish Civil War; the effects of the Second World War (including famines); and the wars in Korea, Vietnam, the Falklands and the Gulf.

Oddly, the archives of the PPU, like the equally informative pacifist archive in the Bodleian Library in Oxford, are not much used by military historians. Likewise, researching conscientious objectors is seldom asked of them. Genealogist Paul Blake, who helped research Claughton Pellew for *The People Detective*, and who specialises in military history, has never before been asked to investigate the subject. It may sound odd to go down the pacifism route in order to find out about war but a great deal can be learnt in this way.

Military Records

What of the people who fought in rather than opposed wars? Research into military records is, of course, a mammoth undertaking and there are whole books devoted to the subject. 'If you're looking for service records after the First World War,' says Paul Blake, 'there's really very little that's easily accessible. From about 1921 onwards you have to contact the Ministry of

Defence – and you have to pay them for information.'

If you want information on soldiers *during* World War One, you're liable to run into problems as well: a vast amount of that material was destroyed by bombing in World War Two. 'About eighty per cent of the records for enlisted soldiers (as opposed to officers) were completely destroyed,' explains Blake. 'Of those that survived, about half were badly damaged and half were perfectly all right. The latter are all available for public inspection, but the former (known as the Burnt Collection) are gradually being released by letters of the alphabet. Roughly two-thirds of the damaged ones are available now.' All the damaged records will, it is estimated, be available by the year 2003. The records for officers (not enlisted men) in the First World War are more or less complete.

Delve back further in time and the search for military records becomes, inevitably, more complicated, especially if your ancestor was an ordinary soldier and not an officer. Prior to the Civil War (1642–9) England had no standing army and regiments were raised only for specific requirements. Few military records survive from this period, although there are some records relating to individuals at the PRO and the Manuscript Department of the British Library. The first full-time trained army dates from the Restoration in 1660 but, again, records at the PRO are few. From1760–1883, you have to know in which regiment your ancestor served because the records (in the form of discharge papers) are archived in regimental sequence.

After 1883, records are arranged separately for the cavalry, infantry, artillery and so on, making one long alphabetical list for the whole army. The papers are fairly detailed and usually give the soldier's place of birth, next of kin, age on enlistment, career summary and details of appearance (to help promote searches should the soldier desert). But they're not complete: prior to 1883, they refer only to those who were discharged on a pension; not to soldiers who deserted or died in action. Officers, however, were not entitled to pensions on retirement until 1871, so if your ancestor was in the commissioned ranks, you'll have to look elsewhere. A huge variety of published lists can be found at the PRO and the SoG, some dating as far back as 1661.

The principal records for officers are the printed Army Lists, which have been published regularly since 1754, and the Regimental Records of Officers' Services, which began in 1775. These are stored at the PRO. So are the Muster Rolls, which generally date from about 1760 to the late 1880s and which contain details of both officers and soldiers who were present at regimental inspections. If you've been unlucky with other sources in tracing an enlisted soldier ancestor, these may be your only source of information, particularly if the soldier in question took an early discharge (i.e. without a pension) or died in service before 1883. But if that's the case, your trawl through the rolls could be very long indeed: one researcher spent fifteen years looking through them to find details of one particular ancestor.

Naval Records

Given that the navy dates back to the time of Henry VIII, that Britannia supposedly ruled the waves for hundreds of years and that, in Nelson's era, the Royal Navy was the biggest employer in the country, there is a pretty good chance that some of your ancestors were seafarers. Happily, there are numerous and wide-ranging accounts about ships and seamen, many of which were written by the sailors themselves. These can be especially interesting as regards building-up a picture of life below decks and on the high seas. In *Ramblin' Jack: The Journal of Captain John Cremmer, 1770–1774*, the author writes of his early days on a ship:

> *Nor could I think what world I was in, whether among spirits or devils. All seemed strange; different language and strange expressions of tongue.*

Captain John Cremmer wasn't the first sailor to regard his profession as peculiar; seamen have always been objects of curiosity, living in an enclosed world on the fringes of society. The ancient Greeks, taking rather an extreme view of their seafaring population, debated whether to count them amongst the living or the dead.

In Britain, naval hierarchy was largely a microcosm of social life, and everyone knew his 'place' in shipboard society. In the broadest possible terms, there were the major hierarchies within a ship's company: officers, ratings (ordinary seamen), marines and servants. Yet within those categories were myriad other distinctions, some of them ill defined, that illustrated the one important difference between the navy and society in general: people were able to rise through the ranks. The position of a midshipman, for example, exemplifies the curious amalgam of official rank and social reality. Midshipmen occupied a limbo between the ranks of officers and ratings: officially they were the latter; they were inferior to warrant officers such as the armourer, sail-maker or cook. Yet, in reality, a warrant officer could be court-martialled for striking a midshipman, suggesting that a midshipman was actually of superior rank. Socially, they usually were: most midshipmen were young gentlemen.

The importance of the navy in previous centuries means that surviving accounts make for fascinating social commentary. And such accounts can be incredibly useful as regards dispelling popular myths. Press gangs, for example, have usually been regarded as the legal equivalent of highwaymen, terrorising the countryside in times of war and forcing all able-bodied men into the navy. While this undoubtedly happened in some instances, the reality was more complex and usually less brutal. Pressing was conducted by the Impress Service, an organisation that dealt with all forms of recruitment (including volunteers), straggling and desertion. While they did raid inns to recruit seamen, most of the inns were near coasts and rivers, where they would be most likely to find men who knew about working on ships and boats. Until Prime Minister William Pitt introduced the Quota Scheme in 1795 (stipulating a certain number of recruits from each English county and port), it was highly unlikely for non-seafaring men to be pressed. It was, after all, in the interests of the navy to recruit men who were, if not exactly willing, at least able.

Food on the ships is another subject that has generated myths. There are enough surviving accounts to dispel the popular notion that life at sea was the equivalent of a floating concentration camp – though eating on the high seas was no picnic; when moored, providing food could be difficult if a ship was in a remote place, but at sea it could be a huge problem.

Breakfast at sea, for instance, came in the rather unappetising form of burgoo, a mixture of oatmeal and water, or 'scotch coffee', bits of burned bread boiled in water and sweetened with sugar.

There were always barrels of salted beef and pork ('stony, fibrous, shrunken, dark and grisly', according to one account) on board ship, but for the majority of a ship's company, fresh meat at sea was a rarity. Officers, however, often had the means to supply their own foodstuffs, turning ships into Noah's Arks in the process. Their meat couldn't have been fresher: cattle, sheep, pigs, goats, hens and geese would have been running around on deck only hours before they were eaten. Some animals were kept as pets: in exotic seas, monkeys, parrots and bears were not uncommon and there is even one account of a French battleship with an elephant on board. But for the men, fresh meat – in the form of fish – was only in regular supply in inland waters, supplemented on the open seas by the occasional dolphin, turtle or seabird.

If your ancestor was an ordinary seaman in the eighteenth and early nineteenth centuries, his living quarters would have been extraordinarily cramped: each seaman had a mere fourteen inches of space for his hammock. In practice, this meant twenty-eight inches, since the occupant of the neighbouring hammock would be on watch while the other was sleeping. The constant damp was another problem and, when a ship was at sea, the gunports in the lower decks had to remain closed, plunging most of the ship's company into permanent twilight.

In 1777, the Admiralty decided that its ships should be healthier, and special air vents were incorporated into the design of new vessels, while hospital ships were assigned to the fleet. Until then, each ship's 'hospital' was the surgeon's cockpit, a grim little hole where operations would be performed with the aid of rum, a leather gag, candlelight and boiling pitch to cauterise amputated limbs. In 1810, the Admiralty went one step further and issued soap as part of a ship's rations.

These are just a few of the countless slices of contemporary life that are divulged in naval accounts. Finding your naval ancestor's name may provide a crucial link in your family tree, but discovering what his life was like can be riveting. But where to look for a naval ancestor? If he was a rating, or ordinary seaman, you may have problems unless you know the name of the ship on which he served. Until 1853, there was no such thing as continuous service for ratings: they were employed on a particular ship and not by the navy. Information about them can be found in the Admiralty Records at the PRO, in naval Muster Rolls which, intriguingly, were introduced by the diarist Samuel Pepys in 1667. Prior to that date, no systematic records survive but you may find mentions of individuals on ships in the Calendars of State Papers, Domestic – again at the PRO. After 1853, the Continuous Service Engagement was introduced and seamen were given numbers and their careers were documented. Their date and place of birth would be recorded, as well as a physical description and a list of the ships in which they served. More detailed information can be found in ships' logs, where every single event on board was recorded.

If your ancestor was an officer you'll find information about him from a rich variety of sources. Records of officers in the navy go back to the Restoration of 1660 and can be found at the PRO. Furthermore, there are numerous lists and publications relating to officers at sea, as well as officers' service records, passing certificates, commission and warrant books. Again, these are in the Admiralty Records at the PRO.

For all naval records after 1924, only the individual to whom they relate, or his next of kin, can apply to view them. Applications should be made to the Ministry of Defence. Other useful sources of information include the Corporation of Trinity House, a charitable foundation founded by Henry VIII in 1514 for the safety, welfare and training of mariners. Records relating to petitions of aid from seamen and their families go back to 1787, and are located in the Guildhall Library.

Further Information

Guildhall Library
Aldermanbury
London EC2P 2EJ
Tel: 020 7332 1868/1870
www.cityoflondon.gov.uk

Imperial War Museum
Lambeth Road
London SE1 6HZ
Tel: 020 7416 5000
www.iwm.org.uk

Ministry of Defence Army & Navy Records Centre
Bourne Avenue
Hayes
Middlesex UB3 1RF
Tel: 020 8573 3831
www.mod.uk

Publications

Commissioned Sea Officers of the Royal Navy (1660–1815), ed.
D. Syrett, Navy Records Society, 1994.

SPENCER FEARON:
Slave Ancestors

The Maroons

❖

Slavery and Slave Records

❖

DNA as a Genealogical Tool

❖

Immigration

Whenever I hear anyone arguing for slavery, I feel a strong impulse to see it tried on him personally.

Abraham Lincoln, 1865

Spencer Fearon is a young black man who dreams of fighting for the British Middleweight boxing title. By an accident of history, he is most likely descended from people who fought and won their freedom from the British over two hundred years ago. Spencer comments: 'Fifty years ago, I wouldn't have been able to fight for the British title. A black man simply wouldn't have been allowed to. So things have changed a lot. I'm British – that's how I think of myself. Even though I'm one hundred per cent British, I'm interested in my roots. I want to know where I come from. I want to know about my family.'

Spencer knew his family came to Britain from Jamaica in the late 1950s, and also knew he was descended from slaves brought to the island sometime in the seventeenth or eighteenth century. He had also been told that his great-great-grandfather was a Maroon, a remarkable community of freed and runaway slaves who established an independent existence in Jamaica in the eighteenth century.

The People Detective took Spencer to Jamaica, to find out more about his roots. Despite regular visits to the island, he had never visited the Maroon villages still in existence in Jamaica, whose traditions and practices mark them out from other Jamaican communities, and connect them to areas in Ghana, West Africa. Nor had he seen the type of country where the Maroons were able to take refuge, and where they ambushed the British expeditions against them.

Spencer gradually found out about the history of his Maroon ancestors and their remarkable guerrilla war against the British. This eventually won them their freedom, land and the right to govern themselves, guaranteed by a treaty in 1738. The treaty stipulated, however, that in exchange for their freedom, the Maroons were required to round up other runaway slaves and return them to their owners. According to Nick Metcalfe, who directed the *People Detective* episode, they often did this so assiduously that they killed the runaways before returning them, which wasn't much use to the planters. 'During slave rebellions,' says Metcalfe, 'they were hired for bounty to hunt down and return the slaves. Apparently, during one rebellion, they brought back just the ears to claim their bounty, but it later emerged they'd cut the ears off dead people. But,' Metcalfe adds, 'the Maroons played it both ways. Often, they would hide runaway slaves as well.'

During his journey, Spencer made the surprise discovery that one of the signatories of the treaty was called Accompong. This name was his original African family name and was an emotional reminder for him of how far back his history went. On reading the treaty, Spencer learnt that, as well as helping to return runaway slaves to the British, the Maroons also helped the British to quell several uprisings by slaves, and even a rebellion in 1865, well after the end of the slave era.

For Spencer, the trip was an extraordinary, emotional voyage of discovery. The distasteful revelation that the Maroons collaborated with the British demonstrates that, sometimes, ancestors did not behave as we would have liked them to; in this case, compromises and sacrifices were made by the Maroons to ensure their freedom.

Spencer's complex search for his roots illustrates that, by and large, researching family history is a luxury limited to white Britons. For black people, there are often two migrations to contend with: one was like that of Spencer's parents, from the Caribbean to Britain in the 1950s or 60s; the other – almost impossible to trace – was the forced migration of slaves from Africa from around 1440 until the abolition of the slave trade in 1807. Everything about the slave trade is unpalatable – especially the grim fact that slaves were regarded not as people but as property. It has been estimated that the continent of Africa lost as many as one hundred million people in the years of the slave trade, all of whom, in turn, lost their identity. It was extremely important for Spencer that *The People Detective*, whilst unable to unearth his African ancestry, uncovered his links with the Maroons.

The Maroons

The original Maroons were African slaves who were imported mainly from the Guinea coast. The Spaniards called them *Cimarrones* (wild cattle) because they were specially trained as trackers and hunters of wild cattle and hogs for the Spanish garrisons and caravans. From the Spanish *Cimarrones* derived the French name *Marrons* and English 'Maroons' (from which, in turn, the word 'maroon' developed, echoing the remote and inhospitable island strongholds occupied by the Maroons).

When some of these slaves escaped in the 1520s, they formed small bands that ruthlessly ransacked Spanish mule trains with their cargoes of gold, silver and supplies for the colonies. Most of the early activities took place in Hispaniola, New Spain and Panama, and in 1553, the first of a series of major uprisings erupted in Nuevo Segovia, Venezuela, with around two hundred and fifty Maroons banding together, electing their own king and a bishop to serve their community. This rebellion was finally crushed by the Spanish military, but only after overcoming stiff resistance.

The most serious revolt of this period occurred in the Darien region of Colombia under a king called Ballano. Ballano and his Maroons posed such a grave threat that the Spanish Viceroy Canete was persuaded to negotiate with them to prevent the escalation of bloodshed. An agreement was signed, giving the Maroons the right to settle as free men under the Spanish law of the West Indies. The terms of this agreement also stipulated that runaway slaves who attempted to join the Maroons should be returned to their masters. The Maroon leader in Hispaniola, Diego de Campo, secured a similar treaty for his group. But despite these treaties, Maroon raids on the Spanish continued. Their ranks swelled as well and, in 1570, there were more than two thousand in the north of Panama.

This was bad news for the Spanish – but a boon for the English privateers who were increasingly sniffing around and pillaging coastal settlements. Francis Drake formed an alliance with the Maroons and, in his notes, described a township of over fifty households living 'civilly and cleanly, and their apparel was very fine and fitly made'.

But it was in Jamaica that the Maroons were most successful. In 1655, pursuing Cromwell's expansionist policies, Britain finally managed to wrest the island from Spanish control. The Spanish Commander Don Cristobal Ysassi retreated to the island's forest-covered hills with a band of slaves who were skilled in tracking and hunting. He effectively used guerrilla warfare to resist the British invasion for some time but, lacking reinforcements, he was eventually forced to abandon his efforts and leave the island. He didn't take his fighting slaves with him: whether this was a deliberate tactic is still a matter of debate. Either way, more slaves subsequently fled to the hills and joined Ysassi's group or formed their own bands. They began attacking the British plantations and settlements and rejected all British efforts to woo them with offers of freedom. Throughout the rest of the 1600s, the Maroons remained ensconced in the inaccessible forests and mountains of Jamaica, from where they continually succeeded in thwarting British attacks.

As sugar supplanted gold as the chief economic base of the West Indies, the strength and frequency of Maroon activity escalated in Jamaica as well as in other Caribbean colonies. The development of sugar plantations necessitated an increasing labour-force, and saw an even greater influx of slaves shipped from Africa, primarily at that time from the areas of the Gold and Ivory Coasts (now Ghana and Côte d'Ivoire). These newly imported Africans were largely Akan-speaking groups and shared a common language with slaves already on the island. This facilitated lines of communication with the Maroons, and saw the formation of alliances that unified and strengthened their efforts. By the 1720s, Maroon hostility had become such a threat to British plantations in Jamaica that many planters were forced to abandon their sugar estates.

On the leeward side of the island, the Maroons were led by Cudjoe, a short, powerfully built man known to be ruthless and brutal yet also considered a peerless master of guerrilla warfare. He was ably assisted by his brothers, Johnny and Accompong. Two other leaders who were noted for their valiant fighting abilities were Cuffee and Quao. On the windward side of the island, the Maroon leader was a sorceress and Obeah woman named Nanny – one of the most notorious captains of the Maroons of that period. The word Nanny may have cuddly connotations for us, but there was nothing nurturing about this Nanny: legend has it that her magic was so powerful that she could attract and catch bullets with her buttocks and render them harmless. This feisty lady is still celebrated in Jamaican folklore, although quite what is fact and what is fiction has been lost to us.

Yet there is nothing fictional about Maroon settlements: as

seen in *The People Detective*, they still survive, testaments to an unbroken thread of history that began nearly four hundred years ago. From the British perspective at the time, the scale of the Maroon problem cannot be overestimated. True, much of the lore may well be just that, but the following document, written in 1734 and unearthed at the PRO by Nick Barratt whilst researching the story, attests to the increasing Maroon threat to the British colony of Jamaica. It is reprinted in full partly because it eventually gave rise to the peace settlement with the Maroons in 1738 (the original treaty can be seen at the PRO), and partly because it is a spectacular example of an official document of the day – spelling inconsistencies and all.

Address of the Governor, Council and Assembly of Jamaica to the King

Wee your Majesties most dutiful and loyal subjects, the Governor Council and Assembly of this your Majestie's Island of Jamaica, are so fully perswaded of your Majestie's tenderness and care for the support and preservation of your people that wee do with the greater assurance and hopes of success, apply to your Majesty to implore your most gracious assistance in our present dangerous and distressed condition. We beg leave to acquaint your Majesty that the danger we are in proceeds from our slaves in rebellion against us, we have for several years past been at an extraordinary and almost unsupportable expense, in endeavouring to suppress them, and whilst we had any reasonable hopes of succeeding wee declined being too importunate for relief, but our attempts against them having been in vain, only convinced us of our weakness, so great that instead of being able to reduce them wee are not in a condition to defend ourselves, the terror of them spreads itself everywhere and the ravages and barbarities they committ have determined several planters to abandon their settlements, the evil is daily encreasing and their success has had such influence on our other slaves that they are continually deserting to them in great numbers and the insolent behaviour of others gives us but too much cause to fear a general defection, which without your Majestie's gracious aid and assistance must render us a prey to them. We humbly beg your Majesty will please to believe our danger at least as great as we represent it and that this may very possibly be the last opportunity we may have of applying for help, but however it may please God to dispose of us, and however miserable our fate may be, wee shall whilst wee have any being wish prosperity to your Majesty and that you may long continue a blessing to the rest of your people.

No wonder Spencer Fearon was proud of the Maroon association. Yet, as seen in the programme, it remains an association – not a proven record. For while Maroon activities were well documented, their genealogies were not.

Slavery and Slave Records

Proud and independent the Maroons may have been, but they were still brought to the island as slaves. And while Jamaica's official written records are comparable in quality to British records made during the seventeenth and through to the twentieth century, slaves were not officially documented until

1817 – ten years after the abolition of the slave trade. There are, at the PRO in London, massive Slave Registers for the whole of the British Empire from 1817–32. A staggering 566 volumes cover the British West Indies, while eighty or so cover Mauritius, and a dozen cover Cape Colony and Ceylon. The volumes contain the name, sex and age (including children) of each individual slave, whether Creole or African; the racial category to which he or she was assigned (negro, mulatto, quadroon etc.), the property on which they lived and the name of their owner. What is interesting is that these volumes are listed under 'T' for Treasury rather than 'CO' for the Colonial Office. Apparently the registers were seen as a prelude to emancipation: the Treasury wanted a record of how many slaves existed but didn't trust the planters to divulge all the details of their 'possessions'. (The details of age and origin influenced the value of slaves.) Thus the census of slaves was bitterly but unsuccessfully resisted by the planters, who realised what it portended.

The extensive records in Jamaica itself date back to the formation of the Island Secretary's Office in 1659, shortly after the island's capture from the Spanish. Despite the ravages of time, hurricanes, fires and earthquakes, continuous colonial rule for three hundred years ensured a fairly good survival rate for the records. In 1879, the Institute of Jamaica was founded in order to care for the island's records and the Archives were established in the 1950s in Spanish Town, the former capital. There, the Island Record Office and the Registrar General's Department house documents copies of baptisms, marriages and burials from the 1660s to the present day. Other records include Patents of Land Grants from

1661–1940, Registers of Returns to Slaves from 1817–1832, accounts of Plantation Expenditure from 1740–1957 and records from the Court of Errors and Court of Appeal from 1709–1838.

In Kingston, the National Library houses an impressive collection of documents including estate maps and unpublished diaries and correspondence throughout the centuries. And those staples of genealogy – photographs and newspapers – are to be found there as well. But perhaps the greatest treasure is a feature known as the Fuertado Manuscripts – fifty-eight volumes of selected bibliographical information on Jamaican worthies from 1655–1870. To quote an article in the *Jamaica Journal* of 1969, the compiler, Walter Augustus Fuertado, 'patiently, year after year, collected snippets of information, put them together and laboriously, volume after volume, transcribed them into a work with a span of over two centuries, a work which is valuable not only as a source of information on individuals, but provides an interesting social history for those who care to read between the lines.'

Yet those researching slave ancestry, like Spencer Fearon, face the often insoluble problem of surnames. Just as members of Scottish clans sometimes took the names of their chiefs, so slaves often appropriated the surname of their owner. Alternatively, they may well have been the biological descendants of their owners. It is common knowledge that practically every white man in Jamaica had a black mistress – and this, sometimes, leads to the unexpected and largely unannounced side of slavery: bequests to black mistresses and their offspring. Copies of wills in Jamaica from as far back as 1660 are available at the Archives in Spanish Town and, as the

People Detective team discovered, they can make for surprising reading. Nick Metcalfe, who directed the Jamaican the *People Detective* episode, recalls: 'There was one instance of a plantation owner leaving £500 to his legitimate family and an estate worth £10,000 to his black mistress. That sort of thing wasn't as uncommon as you might think.' There is another example in the episode itself: an owner declared that his family should not remove anything from his house which his mistress wanted to keep for herself.

'This gave us a glimpse,' says Metcalfe, 'of a world that was fantastically complicated – far more complex than a world of white owners and black slaves. I know it's distasteful to talk about it now, but the gradings – mulattos, quadroons, octoroons – could mean huge differences in status. Some would be free men and others would have held slaves themselves. You couldn't necessarily tell from someone's colour what position they held in life. Nor can you make blanket assertions about plantation owners' relationships with their slaves. We heard of instances of slaves being offered their freedom but refusing to take it. Uncommon, maybe, but it *did* happen.' Not uncommon, however, is the flipside of this. 'It's generally accepted that nearly every black Jamaican will have a white ancestor. What a lot of people don't realise is that nearly every white Jamaican will have a black ancestor.'

But the absence of so many slave records means that, for many, proving ancestry is nigh on impossible. And following the trail back to Africa is simply not an option: you're highly unlikely to find individuals. You might, however, discover an ethnic base.

Gorée Island

No less a personage than Bill Clinton has claimed that Gorée Island, off the coast of Senegal, is 'as much a part of our [American] history as a part of African history'. This is because more than two million slaves passed through Gorée Island, or Isle de Gorée, on their unwilling way to the American colonies between the years of 1680 and 1786. The island – especially after Alex Hailey's controversial book and subsequent series *Roots* – has become a place of pilgrimage for many black Americans. There are any number of travel outfits organising heritage tours to the island, the idea being that black Americans are going back to their roots. Yet this may not necessarily be the case. Gorée was certainly the point of departure for many slaves from Africa, but most of those who sailed from there came from somewhere else.

Furthermore, while the slave trade as we know it appeared with the arrival of the Portuguese in Africa in 1444, slavery itself began centuries before then. One region in Senegal is known to have practised slavery as far back as the eleventh century and, in 1455, Portuguese navigator Ca da Mosto reported that Senegalese King Zucholin: 'maintains his economic power by means of plundering several slaves in both his own country and his neighbours' whom he makes use of, in several ways, mostly in making them cultivate his lands. He sells a good number of those slaves to Arab traders, and also hands some over to the Christians, since the latter started trading with those countries.'

So the slave trade dates, in reality, from much further back than the arrival of the Europeans. No excuse, of course, for the shocking and brutal deportations that deprived Africa of tens of millions of its youngest, fittest inhabitants and caused untold personal misery.

DNA as a Genealogical Tool

It's not just in Jamaica that the history of black people has been poorly recorded. Records in England, until civil registration in 1837, are pretty hopeless: a major oversight (usually due to lack of surnames) considering that the black community in London in the nineteenth century may well have numbered 20,000 – or three per cent of the population. And it can hardly be said that black people were a new phenomenon then: the first black slaves were brought to England in 1440 and there are records of five black men being brought to the country from Africa, by one John Lok in 1555, with the aim of teaching them English so they could act as interpreters in Africa. Look further back in time and you get more of the same: North African legions were stationed here during Roman times and we know that the Phoenicians traded tin with Cornwall and Wales. It's pretty likely that, humans being what they are, these people contributed to the gene pool. So it's not unlikely that many white Britons have black ancestors somewhere along the line.

But that line, more often than not, is far further back than any genealogist or researcher can get to. Until, that is, the recent inception of a project, the Oxford Genetic Atlas (OGA), attempting to chart human history through a genetic 'map'. To date, the project has concentrated mainly on mapping the British Isles – identifying the descendants of Vikings, Saxons and Celts – but, ultimately, it's intended as a global record of all peoples. One black woman, who had always believed that her family originated in Ghana, has learned that she is genetically linked to one of a number of 'maternal ancestors' believed to have lived ten thousand years ago in Kenya. Female ancestry can be established by using mitochondrial DNA (unique in being inherited exclusively through the female line) whilst the Oxford project investigates male ancestry by using Y-chromosome genetic fingerprinting (Y-chromosomes are passed down from father to son, so any male connected to another by paternal links will have identical, or near-identical Y-chromosome fingerprints).

In genealogical terms, this project is still in its infancy, but it has already enabled discoveries to be made that challenge several accepted theories about ethnic divisions, especially in Europe. In simple terms, our current ethnic divisions have little do to with genetics, and a lot to do with religious and political differences. The project is already having immense reper-cussions for the genealogist, as epitomised by its pioneering the recovery of mitochondrial DNA from archaeological bones. The team has established a direct genetic link, for example, between the nine-thousand-year-old 'Cheddar Man' fossil and a teacher who lived down the road from the caves where the fossil was discovered. And we thought we were doing well by tracing our ancestors back to 1837 ...

Another project, led by Dr Ulf Gyllensten of the University of Uppsala in Sweden, and to date the most thorough genetic study of its kind, has traced the human family tree to an 'Eve' who lived in Africa more than fifty thousand years ago. The findings provide the strongest evidence yet that modern humans emerged in Africa relatively recently in the history of evolution before colonising the rest of the world. Using mitochondrial DNA (passed only from mothers) taken from fifty-three men from a range of ethnic backgrounds, the results suggested that the divergence of Africans and non-Africans took place between 52,000 and 28,000 years ago, and was followed shortly afterwards by a population explosion outside Africa. Dr Blair Hedges, an expert in evolutionary genetics at the University of Pennsylvania, commented that 'this date may even be a bit too recent. Other genetic markers indicate an exodus from Africa around 100,000 years ago. But no single genetic marker can time that event precisely, and the mitochondrial date is in the right ballpark.' The 'Out of Africa' theory, however, has its opponents, with other scientists claiming that modern humans evolved simultaneously in Africa, Asia and Europe.

Further information (including DNA testing for family researchers) on the Oxford project can be found at www.oxfordancestors.com on the internet. A sort of 'science made simple' explanation of DNA and genetic research can be found in *The Human Inheritance: Genes, Language and Evolution* (OUP, 1999), edited by Brian Sykes.

Immigration

It's a fairly common misconception that people only began to travel long distances with the advent of railways in the Victorian era. The reality is that they travelled with greater *ease*, but that movement around and between countries has been common since time immemorial. Joseph of Arimathea, so legend has it, travelled from the Middle East to Glastonbury: the debate about that centres around evidence of his ever having been there – not around the possibility of his having travelled thousands of miles in AD 63.

So it is the case with immigrants. As mentioned before, the Phoenicians came to Wales and Cornwall to trade thousands of years ago; as well as probably adding to the gene pool in those regions, there is no reason to suppose that some of their number didn't stay. Immigration has always been with us.

Documentation is a different matter. There is no composite index of names of immigrants to the British Isles over the last thousand years. Finding an exact date is always difficult in the realm of genealogy, but it's not a bad idea to pounce on 1793, when the regulation of aliens arriving in Britain became the responsibility of the Home Secretary. From that date to the present, you're unlikely to go wrong with your research and will, at the PRO, find what you're looking for.

But if you're looking further back, you may still be lucky. The earliest references to aliens resident in England occur in the records of the Chancery and the Exchequer. Again at the PRO, they relate to alien clergy and foreign merchants during the period from Henry III (1216–72) to Henry VIII (1509–47). There are also records, including documents, about the possessions of laymen who were foreign subjects in the period from Edward I (1272–1307) to Edward IV (1422–61). And while the Home Secretary became responsible for the naturalisation of aliens as late as 1844, Acts of Naturalisation dating as far back as 1400 can also be found at the PRO. The Denization Rolls described by Ann Perigo in the Mary Bateman chapter can also be found here, as well as at the Huguenot

Society. The Huguenot Society is an absolute must for information about immigrants; contrary to popular opinion, the Society isn't solely interested in Huguenots: rolls of names of foreigners living in London (and the taxes levied on them) from 1523–61, for example, are to be found there.

Other information at the PRO includes records formerly kept in French, Dutch, German and Swiss churches for refugees in London and other parts of England, and records of French fleeing the revolution from 1789–1814. More modern records (from about 1878) of the Board of Trade contain the names of everyone arriving in the UK from places outside Europe; records that contain the age and occupation of each individual.

Specifics aside, records of immigrants help build up a social and cultural picture of Britain throughout most of the last millennium. There are records of Jewish immigration from 1656 (when Oliver Cromwell revoked the 1290 Edict of Expulsion of Jewry), of Polish, Spanish, Belgian and Hungarian and Czechoslovakian war refugees in the nineteenth and twentieth centuries, and of prisoners of both world wars (although the information here is scant). For those who wish to start tracing their ancestry in what was the British Empire, the huge influx of people from the colonies in the twentieth century can be found in records at the PRO. The Home Office estimates that 160,000 West Indians and over 50,000 migrants from India and Pakistan came to live in Britain from 1955–60. The Immigration Acts of 1962 and 1968 imposed restrictions on what had been a legal right to nationality since 1948, so the tide of migration ebbed. All records are subject to a thirty-year closure rule, so information on the arrival of refugees from Idi Amin's Uganda, for example, will not be available until 2003.

Further Information

Immigration Records
Guildhall Library
Aldermanbury
London EC2P 2EJ
Tel: 020 7332 1868/1870
www.cityoflondon.gov.uk

Bodleian Library
Broad Street
Oxford OX1 3BG
Tel: 01865 277 180
e-mail: www.bodley.ox.ac.uk

Cambridge University Library
West Road
Cambridge CB3 9DR
Tel: 01223 333 000
e-mail: www.lib.cam.ac.uk

Lambeth Palace Library
Lambeth Palace
London SE1 7JU
Tel: 020 7898 1400
e-mail (via the University of London Library) www.ull.ac.uk

Home Office Immigration and Nationality Directorate
3rd Floor
India Building
Water Street
Liverpool
Merseyside L2 0QN
Tel:0151 237 5200
e-mail: www.homeoffice.gov.uk

Museum of Immigration
The Spitalfields Centre
19 Princelet Street
London E1 6QH
Tel: 020 7247 5352
www.nineteenprinceletstreet.org.uk

Jewish Genealogical Society of Great Britain
PO Box 13288
London N3 3WD

Ships' Passenger Lists
www.members.atcanada.ca
This is the work of a private individual, Hugh Reekie, and carries no official imprimatur; it can be quite useful as an index of indexes, however, and points you to various other sources of ships' passenger lists.

GLORIA,
the World's First Supermodel

The Growth of Consumer Culture
✤
The Interwar years

A tale of social history rather than family history, the story of Gloria of Selfridges – probably the world's first 'supermodel' – is a stark contrast to that of the two other hapless women covered in *The People Detective*. A real rags-to-riches story, it's also an example of just how much recent information about an individual can be lost, and subsequently found, with a bit of detection work.

Gloria, christened May Kenworthy, was born in 1905 and died tragically young in 1941. Although she married three times, she had no children, which is probably why her story would have been consigned to the scrapyard of history, had not one John Kenworthy written to *The People Detective* with what little information he knew about her. He, unfortunately, turned out to be no relation to Gloria but, after fairly exhaustive research by genealogist Paul Blake, Clare Cowley, grand-daughter of Gloria's cousin, was located and participated in the series to find out more about her glamorous antecedent.

As for Gloria herself, her life and her achievements were quite extraordinary, given the era in which she was born and grew up. She was born in Delph, near Oldham in Lancashire, and seemed destined to spend her life working in the local woollen mill and adhering to the incredibly strict tenets of the Wesleyan Methodist grandparents who reared her. The political climate of the day certainly wasn't in favour of women branching out to 'do their own thing'. Women were still very much second-class citizens, and were only given the right to vote when Gloria was seventeen (and only then if they were over the age of thirty). It wasn't until 1928 that women were allowed, like men, to vote at the age of twenty-one. It wasn't until 1969 that the voting age for everyone was reduced to eighteen.

There is no evidence to suggest that Gloria was a political animal, but she was certainly an enormous influence on the increasing emancipation of women. As the programme about her life demonstrates, she had a highly public persona. A car, the Triumph Gloria, was said to have been named after her; she was rumoured to have been the model for the Ovaltine girl and, although she was married three times, she was careful to nurture a public image of being a fiercely independent figure.

Her autobiography, serialised in five instalments in the *News of the World* in 1936, demonstrated that she was something of a trailblazer, not just as a fashion icon but also as an independent woman. It also revealed that she wasn't averse to rewriting history – or at least gilding the lily. Gloria never disguised the fact that she came from humble parentage, but she still had delusions of grandeur.

Gloria emancipated herself from the constraints of her

childhood at a very early age. When she was six, her parents separated and, after an itinerant period with her father, she was sent to live with her paternal grandparents who, apart from being fanatically religious, were bigoted and unrelenting in their determination to keep her away from her mother. Until she was thirteen, she attended Delph Council School and then joined the mill as a winder. Clearly this was not the life she envisaged for herself and, after a few months, she ran away to join her mother in Manchester. She must have been a highly determined girl, as running away involved trekking through a snowstorm in the middle of the night to reach the station.

Gloria succeeded in her escape and reached Manchester, where she spent a few months with her mother and younger sister Doris. Although she describes this period as 'rapturously happy', she had obviously decided that she was destined for better things. Mature for her age, she joined a pantomime company as a chorus girl at the age of fourteen. She wrote in the *News of the World*:

> *Chorus girls – or at least a certain type of chorus girl – are pretty hard-boiled, and life in all its crudity was opened up to me. I heard things which made me shudder. I saw things which revolted me, and above all, I learned that a pretty girl must walk warily ... the hardening process begun in the snowstorm had gone on ...*

It was just as well that Gloria became streetwise at such an early age. She subsequently joined a touring company and, when the manager defrauded them after one performance, she ended up at the local parson's house where, to her alarm, he declared his undying love for her. Looking back, however, she wrote:

I am grateful to him to this day, for it was he who caused me to look more intently at my reflection in the mirror. Without any sacrifice of modesty, I knew then I was beautiful.

With this newly acquired knowledge, she began to seek work as a model for women's clothing. The next words in her autobiography are a curious mixture of the coy and the brazen:

Then came a minor success which was to lead to big things. I was photographed for a series of posters for a great firm, whose commodity is world-famous. These posters went all over the country. I took chance by the hand, and determined to go to London. I inserted an advertisement in a personal column, stating 'Gloria has come to London, and would gladly consider any offers. Write Box –'

She was inundated with offers of work, and her career as a mannequin began to take off. But life wasn't without its pitfalls: one day she was assaulted by a hotel manager and, in desperation, stabbed him with a hatpin. Thinking she had killed him, she fled and kept changing her digs for fear of discovery by the police. After three months, she happened to see the hotel manager in the street and, hugely relieved, sought work again at the large fashion houses. In this, she was highly successful and remained at the top of her profession by sacrifices that included giving up smoking, cocktails and going to parties for five years. Today's supermodels would, no doubt, be horrified.

Gloria's really big break came when she was engaged for a huge advertising display at London's Olympia Exhibition Centre. She was approached by a Selfridges employee, who asked if she would like to model at what was arguably the world's most famous and progressive department store. It was to become her 'second home' and, whilst modelling dresses for famous clients there, she met many people and began to be 'fêted quite a lot'. She also began to behave like one of today's supermodels: 'My rules about parties had to be abandoned, so that I spent my evenings at the theatre, the cinema, at the houses of friends, or at decorous dinners.'

Curiously, Gloria married the most unlikely of her admirers; an electrician whom she merely refers to as 'George', adding that 'for reasons which will become obvious I cannot give his surname'. Quite what those reasons were never did become clear, but the George in question was one George Harry Pizer, whom she married on 4 September 1926. The marriage certificate was obtained by Paul Blake, who helped research this episode.

The marriage was a disaster and Gloria went to work in Paris in the most successful salon of the day: Jenny Dolly's on the Champs-Elysées. Her autobiography becomes quite racy when she recalls those days and there is a roll call of dukes, duchesses and other assorted aristocrats, including the King of Spain, who made her acquaintance. She claims her fan mail: 'became so voluminous that I had to seek help to cope with it,' and says that she was recognised wherever she went. Interestingly, she never gave her full name to anyone. A precursor to some of today's celebrities, she remained just 'Gloria'.

In the *News of the World*, Gloria refers to several attempted assaults, to a scandal about a supposedly 'nude' portrait of her, and to various pieces of gossip of the day. Her words are never sensational, but it is clear that she (or more probably her editor) was intent on causing a sensation. As the newspaper instalments continue, we learn of the '4000 friends' Gloria made during her modelling career; of the 60,000 times she posed for photographs; of the heir to a title whom she loved and would have married had his family not objected to her being 'only a model'; and of an attempt to force her to model highly revealing underwear. Gloria goes on to refer to her cruises in the Mediterranean, holidays in French châteaux, 'thousands' of marriage proposals and, of course, to the fashions of the day. It's all pretty frothy stuff.

Gloria doesn't refer much to her work at Selfridges although, in the final newspaper instalment, she does mention the extraordinarily innovative Husband's Advisory Bureau run by the store. Gloria was one of the 'front-women' for this service, which provided harassed husbands with ideas on what to give their wives as presents. It seems pretty tame stuff by today's standards, but it was part of the reason why Selfridges wasn't just a shop but a revolutionary shopping experience, special-ising in the all-but-unheard-of area of customer relations. Today, people take it for granted that shopping is an experience but, as seen in the *People Detective* episode on Gloria, this concept was really invented at Selfridges.

At the time that Gloria's *News of the World* autobiography was published, she was still working at Selfridges but left later that year, with fellow mannequin Dawn Dickens, to set up her own mannequin school. On 16 January the following year she got married for the second time, to one Albert Gordon Jackson, a film production manager. He died in 1940 and, that same year, on 1 June, she married Cecil Edward Lane, a totaliser supervisor who was also a second lieutenant in the armed forces.

The following year, on 5 June, Gloria died of barbiturate poisoning. She was found after five days at her home in West London and was identified at the inquest by her husband. The verdict was recorded as open, although suicide was widely suspected at the time. In one of her obituaries, a neighbour is quoted as saying: 'She was still very beautiful and appeared quite happy but her life had been saddened by domestic illness.' It is also not unlikely that it had been saddened by her third marriage. Most of her friends and family were unaware that she had married Cecil Lane, and he appears to have been a particularly shadowy figure. There were even strong rumours that he had murdered Gloria for her money. He died in 1966.

In researching Gloria's life, *The People Detective* found that her relative, Clare Cowley, knew very little about her. It was difficult to locate Clare in the first place, as Gloria had no direct descendants of her own. However, the purpose of the initial research conducted by Paul Blake was firstly to verify Gloria's own birth, marriages and antecedents and then to search all avenues for people related to her.

This research was not helped by Gloria's title throughout her life of 'the mystery mannequin'. In the final instalment of her autobiography, Gloria promises to reveal everything about herself, but this is where the humble May Kenworthy gets something of a makeover, and Gloria still doesn't mention her original Christian name, or her uninspiring background.

As her descendant, Clare Cowley, discovered when she 'relived' Gloria's life in *The People Detective*, the contrast between the woollen mills of Gloria's childhood and the gilded salons and glittering gowns of her later life (which Clare modelled in the programme) was staggering. Gloria, however, implied that the contrasts were not so great. She tells us that the Kenworthys had lived in Delph for 'centuries' and that her father was a successful contractor and at times held important positions. This may well have been true, but on his marriage certificate, Gloria's father listed his profession as 'joiner' – hardly the mark of a master builder!

Gloria really gets into her stride with the following extract from the *News of the World*:

> *Way back in the family was a connection with the great*
> *Strabolgi family and as a girl I was told something about the*
> *two branches of the family reaching an irrevocable breach*
> *because of one side being Whig and the other Tory. The*
> *Strabolgi barony was created in 1381 and has centuries of*
> *association with Yorkshire.*

The People Detective tried to discover whether there were any grand associations amongst Gloria's antecedents. They found instead that her ancestors were a collection of joiners, bleachers and weavers. Gloria wasn't the first and will by no means be the last person to inject a bit of lustre into her family tree – and who can blame her? It's a long way from a Lancashire woollen mill to the world of the beautiful people and the front pages of the world's press.

The research involved in finding Gloria's descendant, Clare Cowley, is actually a good example of how much information has to be sifted through in order to find a family connection that, in genealogical terms, doesn't go back very far. The research wasn't helped by the fact that Gloria's younger sister, Doris, married aged nineteen but produced no children.

Paul Blake extended his net far and wide, searching records over more than a century to find out more about Gloria. Below is an extract from his researches: stage one out of four stages. Anyone interested in employing a professional genealogist may like to know that they would receive a similar sort of outline, although it should be emphasised that there is no such thing as a standard genealogist's report – it very much depends on the client's brief :

Stage One

Certificates obtained:
Birth of May KENWORTHY, 8 February 1905, Beswicks, Delph; daughter of Albert and Emma (née PENDLEBURY), Joiner.

Marriage of George Harry PIZER, Electrician, and May KENWORTHY, 4 September 1926 at Marton in Craven. At this time, May was living in Marton in Craven.

Marriage of Albert Gordon JACKSON, Film Production Manager, and May otherwise Gloria PIZER formerly KENWORTHY, the divorced wife of George Henry PIZER, 16 January 1937 at Paddington Register Office.

Marriage of Cecil Edward LANE, Totalisator Supervisor, and Gloria May JACKSON, widow, 1 June 1940 at St Marylebone Register Office.

Death of Gloria May LANE, 5 June 1941, of barbiturate poisoning.

Marriage of Albert KENWORTHY, Joiner, age 21, of Heys, Delph, son of John KENWORTHY, Weaver, and Emma PENDLEBURY; on 26 March 1904 at Friar-Mere.

Birth of Albert KENWORTHY, 19 July 1882, Heys, Saddleworth; son of John and Hannah (née BROADBENT), Farmer.

Newspaper reports obtained:
News of the World, *21 December 1941*
The Times, *7 November 1941*

Census Return entries obtained:
1891 Census of Heys, Saddleworth, for John and Hannah KENWORTHY and family, including ALBERT, aged 9.

1881 Census of Heys, Saddleworth, for John and Hannah KENWORTHY and family.

Subsequent stages of research involved: searching for remarriages of Gloria's first and third husbands (her first husband remarried and had four children); obtaining wills and the addresses of people mentioned in them; researching Gloria's only sister and looking for any children from her marriage (there were none). Interestingly, Paul Blake's research also involved checking that Gloria didn't have any children herself. Genealogists constantly repeat the phrase: 'people don't always tell the truth' and, although Gloria claimed she didn't have any children, for whatever reason, this may not have been true. As far as could be ascertained, however, she was indeed childless.

The Growth of Consumer Culture

Gloria doesn't say much about Selfridges and nothing at all about Gordon Selfridge in her autobiography. This is a pity because his is the story of an American who transformed the face of shopping in Britain and, arguably, the world. It was his pioneering attitude towards consumer culture that helped women such as Gloria lead the emancipated lifestyles they so cherished.

Although it is a myth that women did not travel or shop on their own before the twentieth century (respectable Victorian women often travelled alone on the London underground), Gordon Selfridge had extraordinarily advanced ideas about the role of women in society, both as customers and as employees. He realised that more and more women were gaining independence, and encouraged them all the way. He sent his female staff on training courses in the United States, established a sales assistant school and a staff council and helped transform the role of the clothes mannequin from that of a static clotheshorse into a personality. He also had an uncanny knack for wooing the public: for the campaign to announce the opening of Selfridges on 15 March 1909, none of the adverts had anything to do with selling; they were all about instilling a public perception of the store's solicitous attitude to its customers.

Harry Gordon Selfridge was born in 1856 into a small, straitlaced community of the Midwest in Ripon, Wisconsin. Of Scottish descent through the male line, he inherited both the Protestant work ethic and the Midwestern attitude to endeavour and hard graft. His mother was particularly influential in his life, always inspiring him, raising his ambitions and encouraging him to imagine what he could do if he were rich. He certainly wasn't born into wealth, and suffered early in life with the death of his father, a storekeeper, in the Civil War, followed a few years later by the death of his brother.

Selfridge's working life began at the age of eleven, delivering papers and bread. He subsequently moved on to become an office boy in a bank, a bookkeeper in a furniture factory and a clerk in a small insurance company. At the age of twenty-three, he moved to Chicago in search of better opportunities. He found them. Whilst working for the department store Marshall Field's, he learned lessons that shaped his career and, later, made him his fortune.

Selfridge realised that the tastes of the buying public were being arbitrarily decided by the wholesale men and that people's real needs and wants were being ignored. Wholesale dictated to retail: Marshall Field's attitude was that the latter had no future. Selfridge thought otherwise. He believed the two sides should be working together, both creating demands and supplying them. He also believed in radical principles such as the value of good publicity, and he promoted many store practices that still exist today, more than a century later. Selfridge devised the concept of a 'greeter' to meet ladies from their carriages; he discarded high shelves which previously had to be reached by step-ladder, and displayed goods on counters where they could be seen; he is also credited with developing modern store lighting.

Other innovations included making way for new stock by having annual sales, inventing the 'bargain basement' by generating turnover from piles of stuff abandoned in the basement, and inspiring the first full-page adverts in the Chicago newspapers. He made news out of shopping, even linking the firm's publicity with local election campaigns (something he did to great effect at Selfridges when he promoted general elections). Many people at Marshall Field's saw him as a 'cheapening influence' on the firm, but he was the one who abolished the word 'cheap' from the shop's windows and substituted it with 'less expensive'.

Perhaps Selfridge's greatest gift was as a keen social observer. He realised that women were becoming increasingly emancipated and did everything he could to encourage this shift in the social balance. Indeed, he later claimed that he had helped with the emancipation of women: 'They came to the store and realised some of their dreams.' He opened a tearoom on the third floor after a customer complained of not being able to get 'a glass of milk and a bun', and he followed this with a series of restaurants on the seventh floor. He opened a glove cleaning and children's wear department so that women could meet, whether they came as shoppers or not.

Selfridge remained at Marshall Field's for twenty-five years, and had an indisputable impact on the balance sheet. When he was not planning new departments, he was introducing new methods into the 'counting-house' and devising new advertising strategies and slogans – like 'X shopping days until Christmas'. He was one of the original practitioners, if not the inventor, of the 'ethical strategy' by which modern advertising influenced not just customers but whole communities. He despised aggressive approaches in advertising and preached honesty with efficiency, profits with dignity.

Selfridge outstripped all of his contemporaries at Marshall Field's and, in 1890, he became a junior partner, earning $20,000 a year. Now wealthy enough to travel, he toured Europe, admiring amongst other sights, Paris's Bon Marché, the world's first department store. On his return, he married Rose Amelia Buckingham, a débutante whose father came from the highest social circle of Chicago. The wedding was a lavish society affair, and they were married for thirty years, producing four children.

By the time Selfridge left Marshall Field's in 1904, the retail profit touched an unprecedented $1,445,000. Although he was nearly fifty, he still had enormous enthusiasm and zest for life and, deciding to strike out on his own, he moved to New York and bought the store Schlesinger and Mayer. However, he sold it after three months and decided to 'retire' to his sumptuous abode on Lake Geneva, seventy miles from Chicago.

But Selfridge was designed to be an innovator. He also had itchy feet and, believing London to be the greatest city in history, moved across the Atlantic in 1906. There he visited the large department stores of Harrods, Debenhams and Dickens and Jones, and found them 'soundly established' but not very inspiring. Summarising his London impressions, he declared that 'they know how to make things in England, but not how to sell them'. So he told them how to do it. Three years after arriving in the capital, he opened what is still one of its greatest department stores: Selfridges.

As seen in the *People Detective* episode, Selfridges caused a sensation when it opened in 1909; nothing like it had ever been seen in London. The store had its own library, post office, American soda fountain and silence room, where a sign read: 'Ladies will refrain from conversation'. Innovations were constantly introduced: Selfridges was the first store to extend credit and to mount exhibitions: one, of the latest scientific discoveries, led to the world's first television sales department. Another department, following Amy Johnson's epic flight to Australia, was opened to sell aeroplanes.

Gordon Selfridge's staff recruitment techniques were typically radical too. He imported his top staff from the US, but left them to express themselves in their own domains, subject only to the 'policy of the house', which he dictated himself. Huge queues of applicants for jobs in the 130 departments lined the side-streets and 10,000 people were interviewed. Selfridge told his staff director to find out 'something about the family circumstances' of each applicant, hinting that of the female hopefuls, preference should be given to those who would make 'good mothers'. He even went as far as to instruct his staff director to tour the best girls' schools in London to look for suitable junior female candidates. And he sent his buyers off to find the best goods, fashions and ideas in design and presentation on the Continent and in the US.

By the time Gloria came to Selfridges, the store was the undisputed leader of London's department stores. Indeed, it had its heyday in the 1930s, partly because Selfridge himself continued to capitalise on, and influence, cultural shifts. He also continued to woo women as his most important customers. He was helped in this by the hugely glamorous Hollywood films of the era and the emergence in the interwar period of female entrepreneurs selling their products to women. Elizabeth Arden and Helena Rubenstein were amongst their number. So, too, on the couture side, was Coco Chanel. Other, subtler developments were not lost on Selfridge; 'women's fiction', by the likes of Agatha Christie, emboldened female customers to experiment with up-to-the-minute fashions and cosmetics and the increasing glamorisation of the colonies influenced the ever-changing design of the store. Tearooms, for example, were awash with palms and other exotic artefacts in order to give consumers the impression that they were living out their fantasies at the top of the colonial tree.

Gloria was fortunate to be able to live out her fantasies amongst the beau monde of Europe. So, too, was Gordon Selfridge; the boy from the Midwest mixed with the great and the good of the day and became an establishment figure. While Gloria never managed to bag the jewel in the crown of family history: a title, two of Selfridge's daughters did. Beatrice became the Comtesse de Sibour and Rosalie, the Princess Wiasemsky. But Selfridge himself did manage to square his own genealogical circle: he recaptured his Scottish ancestry by becoming a British citizen in 1937.

The Interwar Years

The People Detective discovered some intriguing aspects of social history while they were researching Gloria's life. The interwar period is one of the most fascinating, and overlooked, eras of social history. It is particularly interesting when one considers the story of Gloria and the role of women in society. 'Official' recognition of women's rights came at the end of the First

World War, when women over the age of thirty were given the right to vote. In reality, women had started to play an increasingly influential role in society by being 'war workers' in factories and hospitals during the war; the war may have ended in 1918 but the liberation of women was only just beginning.

In tandem with this change came another massively influential development in British society: the influx of Americans. Wealthy American tourists started to flock to Europe almost as soon as the Armistice was signed and, although France and Italy were the preferred destinations, a visit to Britain was usually on the agenda as well. Their impact was momentous, especially in the areas of women's cosmetics and fashion. Although women had been using face powder for centuries, there had been very little advance since then. With the arrival of American tourists, this was to change for ever. The Americans brought with them a host of unfamiliar fashions, amongst them lipstick, rouge and eyebrow and eyelash colouring. These products had hitherto been unheard of in Britain, as had the phenomenon of the beauty parlour.

As for clothing, the most important and lasting development was the abandonment of the whale-boned corset. Although women war workers had already dispensed with this stiff and uncomfortable item that, in the main, they had worn since the age of thirteen, others only began to do so with the arrival of their American counterparts. American women had long enjoyed less social restraint than British women, and their arrival on these shores, coupled with the cessation of hostilities, was crucial to the permanent changes that were now developing.

The war had seen, for practical reasons, the widespread

adoption of short hair and short skirts ('short', however, was a relative term: a skirt was considered short if it revealed the ankle). Rather than revert to pre-war fashions, women realised the benefits offered by less restrictive wear, and something of a revolution now began. This is perhaps best epitomised by the image of the 'flapper' of the 1920s: cropped hair, cloche hat, short sleeves and, for the racier of their number, trousers during the day. Counterpoint that image against the Edwardian look of ten years previously, with layer upon layer of full-length clothes, and it becomes clear that fashion had indeed been subject to a momentous revolution.

Perhaps most revolutionary of all was the woollen jumper. It might sound tame today, but it was the subject of much discussion, and some outrage, that both women and men began to wear this interchangeable garment. Jumpers were previously only worn by little boys and (in white) by sportsmen. But now women, relieved of the burden of knitting socks for soldiers, began to make jumpers for themselves and, subsequently, for their menfolk. Lest they be accused of wearing girly garments, men called their jumpers 'pull-overs'.

It is interesting (and highly relevant today) that the interwar period provoked much discussion about the changing roles of the sexes and the emasculation of men. Not only did women look different, but they also acted differently. In the 1920s, women started to smoke in public, dance to jazz music (with what was considered in some quarters to be 'shameless abandon') and to frequent public houses. Furthermore, they began to populate areas that had previously been regarded as the domain of the male. More and more women took up some sort of profession; a task made easier by the Sex Disqualification

(Removal) Act of 1919, which admitted women to hitherto male professions, including the law. The first woman barrister was called to the bar in 1921, and another thirty were called in 1922. University, too, became an option after Oxford admitted women to full membership in 1919.

Numerous other measures ensured the increasing emancipation of women. The first woman to sit in Parliament, in 1919, was the indomitable – and American – Nancy Astor and, shortly thereafter, several acts were passed to alter the legal position of women in society. In 1923, for example, the Matrimonial Causes Act meant that adultery of either spouse could be sufficient reason for divorce: previously, women (but not men) had also to prove cruelty or desertion. Two years later, the Criminal Justice Act provided another landmark for women's independence: it did away with the presumption that a woman who committed a crime in the presence of her husband did so because he urged her to.

Hand in glove with changes in the law came changes in attitudes – particularly to sex. In the 1920s, Dr Marie Stopes pioneered the widespread use of contraceptives and the increasingly open attitude towards them. It was she who inaugurated the first birth-control clinic in London's East End; a much-needed institution given the extreme reluctance of doctors of the day to advise women on contraception. Shifts in the sexual code extended to new attitudes on divorce. Again, this also had something to do with the influx of Americans, who took much more liberal views on the subject. Their view was that an unhappy marriage was a problem that could be solved: not a life-long sentence of misery. Furthermore, divorce in the States, amongst the more affluent sections of society, carried little social stigma and, by the 1920s, divorce amongst upper-class Britons was almost regarded as fashionable. It was certainly widely talked about. The plays of Noël Coward, for example, revel in the matrimonial musical chairs.

American influences spread everywhere, and not all of them were laudable. In the popular press, for example, journalists followed the examples set across the water and became increasingly unscrupulous in seeking out stories. People's private lives were regarded as legitimately up for grabs, and papers paid small fortunes to seek out scoops. Lurid crime stories became increasingly fashionable, as did 'sensations'. Perhaps the biggest and certainly the most enduring sensation, was the advent of the Loch Ness monster. The craze began in 1933 and led to an unstoppable flow of stories about the nature and activities of the creature in the loch. The baton was also picked up by foreign papers: a Japanese paper declared that the monster roamed over the heath where Macbeth had consorted with the three witches. On April Fool's Day in 1936, a German paper announced that the beast had been captured and was on exhibition in Edinburgh.

More serious American imports, and ones that Gordon Selfridge capitalised on, came in the form of increased mechanisation, and affected every area of life. Cigarette machines, lunch and fruit machines began to appear in the streets and, in shops and restaurants, mechanical gadgets became all the rage. Even the restaurant itself became 'mechanical' with the advent of the American-style cafeteria. This involved the novel concept of queuing up with a tray and passing in front of a chrome counter, where ready-to-eat dishes were laid out.

Although big stores such as Selfridges and Woolworths were quick to introduce cafeterias, they didn't catch on as quickly as that other 'new' way to eat: at a milk bar. These were hugely popular alternatives to the traditional and rather dowdy tea shops and became widespread during the 'Drink More Milk' campaign of the 1920s. Milk bars were normally light and bright, with large expanses of glass and chrome and high stools and counters. Their design, which was usually open on the street side, encouraged people to frequent them when time was short. People used them at lunch breaks or before the theatre or cinema, dropping in to sample milk-based drinks with wacky names that, moreover, were supposed to be good for you. Before the war, no one except the very young and the very ill drank milk: now, it was the height of fashion.

One mechanical invention that had been around for some time was the motor car. In the 1930s, however, the press began to print stories about its pernicious influence on public safety. Around 7000 people a year died from accidents involving cars, and another 100,000 were injured. The government, quick to react to press agitation, embarked on a road-safety campaign in 1934. New road signs were introduced, more roundabouts and traffic lights were built and, to avoid congestion in crowded or narrow roads, one-way streets were also introduced. One of the most visible changes effected by Leslie Hore-Belisha, the Minister of Transport, was to mark pedestrian crossings with black-and-white lines and put orange beacons on the pavement to indicate their presence. These were, and still are, known as Belisha beacons.

Some of Belisha's other reforms were regarded as nothing short of radical. It was he who was responsible for the driving test: before 1934 absolutely anyone could get a driving licence without even demonstrating knowledge of how to operate a car. Another motoring revolution came with what were known as 'courtesy cops': policemen whose specific role was to drive around and warn motorists of any infringement of the new laws; amongst them breaking the thirty-mile-an-hour speed limit in built-up areas. (Elsewhere, people could drive as fast as they wanted.) Belisha's innovations appeared to have been highly effective: despite the fact that more and more cars were coming on to the road, there was a marked decrease in the number of road accidents by the end of the year.

The 1930s also saw developments of interest to the family researcher as well as the social researcher. Medical research made massive improvements in the treatment of various diseases, especially in venereal diseases. It also saw the beginning of blood transfusion and, by the late thirties, heightened interest in what the newly-discovered blood groups could reveal. It was found that children inherited the characteristics of their parents' blood groups and this, in turn, meant radical advances in establishing paternity. If a child had blood-group charac-teristics which neither parent possessed, then there had obviously been a third party involved. Blood tests therefore became useful in determining paternity cases in court; although a blood test couldn't provide proof that a man was the father of a particular child, it could prove that he wasn't. Newspapers, of course, were quick to seize upon this new sensation and exploited it to the full by reporting such court cases.

There was, during this period, something of a national obsession with health and well-being, and social research groups began publishing information about the nation's health.

Their intention was to provide local and national authorities with reference works about social questions, but the knock-on effects were far more wide-ranging. The press and the public began to take an interest and books on social history became popular. This, in turn, led to the birth of market research into lifestyle. Advertising agencies started to employ girls (they were always female, as people responded more readily to their questioning), to conduct door-to-door questioning about what people wanted out of life and what products would make them feel better. The agencies were subsequently able to inform their clients about what the public wanted, and what form of advertising would most readily make them respond. This sort of information was eagerly devoured by retailers like Gordon Selfridge.

The first major opinion polls were conducted in America by a Dr Gallup and his American Institute of Public Opinion, and reached these shores in 1936. Here, it was entitled 'Mass Observation' and resolved to find out what people thought about just about everything. Market research did, however, have its detractors, who felt that it heralded a dangerous onslaught on privacy. The press pounced on this and declared that it was insidious 'Mass Eavesdropping', also ridiculing its claim to be a science. Nevertheless, the masses constantly talked about it and, almost overnight, it became a social phenomenon. It was also, arguably, the start of spin-doctoring: if you knew what people wanted to hear or have, you could give it to them. Or, more pertinently, you could pretend that you were going to give it to them.

One of the most popular activities of the interwar years was a sedentary one: 'listening-in' to the radio or, as it was then called, the wireless. The apparatus had been of immense service in naval warfare during the Great War and, subsequently, developed into a popular news and broadcast service. 1919 saw the birth of large-scale transmission under the aegis of the Marconi Company and, in 1922, the Postmaster-General gave the green light to public service broadcasting, allowing the formation of the BBC (the British Broadcasting Company, now the British Broadcasting Corporation).

Typically, Gordon Selfridge made much of the new invention. In 1923, the BBC asked him if masts for its station could be installed on the roof of his store. He agreed, and two 150-foot towers were erected, and continued in operation until 1929. In 1924, he installed nineteen speakers inside the store, in order to let shoppers hear, for the first time, the voice of King George V when he opened the British Empire Exhibition at the newly built Empire Stadium at Wembley. Some customers, over-awed by the occasion, stood to attention as they listened.

But it was Gordon Selfridge's son who evinced interest in the next new invention and gave it publicity within the store. He had heard of the experiments of one John Logie Baird and, fascinated by what he called a 'televisor', tracked him down to Soho and offered him £25 a week to demonstrate his apparatus three times a day in the store and to answer customers' questions. The impecunious Baird agreed with alacrity but, after three weeks in the electrical section of Selfridges, his distaste for public performance became apparent and he resigned. Although customers had expressed interest in the indistinct black-and-white images of various objects, few understood the impact that 'television' would have. Even newspapers of the day regarded it as a cheap novelty, with only the *Daily Telegraph* commenting of the new exhibit at Selfridges that it would be of 'historic memory' in years to come. In Selfridges itself, only the founder agreed. To his dismissive Sales Manager, he cautioned: 'This is not a toy, Williams. It is a link between all peoples of the world. Great good can come of it.' Prescient words indeed. Yet it wasn't until 1939 that television became widely recognised as a viable and workable invention.

Until then, radio ruled the airwaves. Indeed it was seen by some as crucial to society and, in particular, to education. By the end of the 1920s, some 11,000 schools were listening-in to educational talks provided by the BBC. Newspapers, however, were highly critical of the BBC, complaining that the voices of the announcers were too refined and the talks too dull. The dramas were also criticised – for being 'too exciting'. Much of the criticism was levied because newspaper proprietors, understandably, felt that the BBC was encroaching on their territory. The BBC itself understood this and, in its early days, agreed not to broadcast news between midnight and 6pm. Nor did it give running commentaries on sporting events. But when the BBC became a public corporation in 1927, the rules were relaxed and daytime news commentaries began to appear.

One of the most popular pastimes amongst the well heeled in the 1930s was flying. Gordon Selfridge, as ever, was quick to capitalise on this and opened an aviation department in Selfridges. The popularity of aeroplanes was largely due to Amy Johnson becoming, in 1930, the first women to fly solo to Australia. Look deeper, however, and you find a more complex, triangular relationship between the popular crazes and sensations (like flying), the press and men like Selfridge who were lightning-quick to respond to such new trends.

Amy Johnson was in many ways a creation of the *Daily Mail*. The paper had, since the late 1920s, been offering cash prizes for people who flew to remote or far-flung places. For her nineteen-day flight to Australia, Johnson won the enormous sum of £10,000 from the *Mail* and, after her return, the paper celebrated her with a banquet attended by London luminaries as well as leading women achievers in all walks of life. She was then sent around Britain on a flying tour to celebrate her achievement – a mission that handily also served to advertise the *Mail*.

Selfridge was one of the distinguished guests at the banquet in London. Although Johnson's flight took place in May, he had pre-empted the furore that would surround it by opening Selfridges aviation department in April. The ensuing publicity for the store was, of course, immense. As indeed it was for Amy Johnson. She delighted her public by marrying an ex-Royal Air Force pilot and, for the next seven years, they lived their lives under intense media scrutiny as they vied with each other to break more aviation records. Hounded by the new-style American 'news hawks', they suffered the indignity of endless and, to modern readers, now-familiar untruths being printed about them until, in 1938, their marriage was dissolved.

One family was still exempt from salacious stories in the press: the royal family. This, however, was a relatively recent phenomenon, dating from around the turn of the century. Prior to that (and especially back in the Regency period) the royal family was regarded as fair game and pot shots were aimed at them from all directions. (One of the last recorded remarks against them was a tongue-in-cheek statement in an 1890s sport sheet: 'There is nothing whatever between the Prince of

Wales and Lillie Langtry. Not even a sheet.') The respectful
silence of the early twentieth century was, however, sorely tried
by the crisis that nearly toppled the monarchy: the story of
Edward and Mrs Simpson.

The public at large knew nothing about Mrs Simpson and
remained generally adoring of their new king. After all, he was
good-looking, encouraged the pursuit of fitness (a great thirties
fad), was known to be affable and, for at least ten years, had
done much to popularise men's fashion. Sometimes he shocked
the public with his outré tastes, yet even his more unconven-
tional fashions would filter down to his subjects. He, more than
anyone else, influenced men to wear shorts, slacks, open-necked
shirts, Tyrolean hats and bright colours.

The story of Edward VIII's liaison with Wallis Simpson, long
known to high society, the Cabinet and latterly the Church,
began to leak to the press in early December 1936. The story
quickly escalated into tales of a terrible constitutional crisis,
fuelled by the fact that Mrs Simpson was twice divorced and that
the king wasn't a regular church-goer. Most of the populace at
large appeared to side with the king, but this didn't really
matter. The Government was set against his marrying the
woman he loved and, on 10 December, he capitulated to
parliamentary and family pressure and, that afternoon, Prime
Minister Stanley Baldwin read the message of abdication in the
House of Commons. The ex-king, now Prince Edward (although
he had actually been christened David), broadcast his own
abdication speech to the nation that night. He left for Europe the
next morning.

The result, of course, was that his younger brother George
(christened Albert) became king and the nation cheered once

more. So, presumably, did Gordon Selfridge. The coronation of King Edward had been planned for 12 May 1937 so, stepping neatly into the breach, the new king's coronation was set for the same day. Selfridge had already made great plans for how his store would celebrate the coronation, with plans budgeted at £25,000 (well over half a million pounds today). Now, because a different brother with a different name was about to assume the throne, everything had to be altered and it ended up costing Selfridge around £50,000.

All the great London stores tried to trounce each other in the magnificence of their banners, bunting, acres of red, white and blue flowers and massive statues and placards of the royal family. By common accord, Selfridges was deemed the most opulent, not to say expensive.

An Indian rajah, in town for the event, fell in love with the decorations, bought and dismantled them (this took six weeks), and reassembled them in his own palace. The author E. M. Forster saw them and was less impressed, pronouncing them 'Awful!' But Gordon Selfridge's excessive display of patriotism probably had an added agenda: although he had already applied for naturalisation as a British subject, he was still an American citizen. In June that year, however, he was granted his British passport.

Further Information

History of Advertising Trust
Hat House
Raveningham Centre
Raveningham
Norwich NR14 6NU
Tel: 01508 5486623

Newspaper Archives
Bodleian Library
Broad Street
Oxford OX1 3BG
Tel: 01865 277180
www.bodley.ox.ac

British Library Newspaper Library
Colindale Avenue
London NW9 5HE
Tel: 020 7412 7353
www.bl.uk

National Library of Ireland
Kildare Street
Dublin 2
Tel: 00 3531 603 0200
www.heanet.ie/natlib/

National Library of Scotland
Department of Manuscripts
George IV Bridge
Edinburgh EH1 1EW
Tel: 0131 226 4531
www.nls.uk

National Library of Wales
Department of Manuscripts and Records
Penglais
Aberystwyth
Ceredigion SY23 3RU
Tel: 01970 632 8000
www.llgc.org.uk

FLORENCE MAYBRICK,
the Notorious Poisoner

Jack the Ripper

♣

Royalty, the Aristocracy and Heraldry

The city of Liverpool has long had connections with the southern states of America. Cotton trading provided the greatest link between them and, to illustrate just how strong the connection was, Confederate flags flew in Liverpool during the American Civil War.

Another link, which caused a nationwide outcry, provided the background for this episode of *The People Detective*: the episode tracing the tragic history of southern belle Florence Maybrick, accused of poisoning her cotton trader husband in Liverpool, and sentenced to death by hanging. Such was the paucity of evidence against her, the case would, nowadays, probably not even have made it to court. Even in 1889, when the trial took place, it was widely considered to have been a travesty of justice.

The story of Florence Maybrick was, and is, a classic Victorian melodrama. It began when the young Florence

Chandler sailed with her mother to England. This type of voyage was common with many southern girls of impeccable breeding, and seems to have had no other purpose than that of finding Florence a husband. Her mother had already had some practice in that quest. Her own first two husbands had died prematurely and her third and last, the Baron von Rocques, may have had a title but he was a bully and abusive towards his wife. Florence, apparently, spent her formative years in the care of nannies – a hostage to her mother's instability, financial insecurity and lack of sound values. The fact that she had gone through most of her childhood and adolescence without any sort of authority figure may have had an effect on her behaviour in later years. She was, by all accounts (especially those at her trial), rather flirtatious. She may, of course, just have been practising what she had learned from her mother. Or, more likely, behaviour that was normal in Alabama didn't sit well in prudish Victorian England.

But Florence didn't have to wait until reaching England (or their final destination – Paris) to find a husband. She met James Maybrick on the voyage to Liverpool on the SS *Baltic* in 1880. She was just eighteen; he was forty-two. Born in Liverpool in 1839, Maybrick was the son and grandson of parish clerks of the fashionable city church of St Peter's. He had a conventional secondary-school education and, aged twenty, entered a ship-broker's office in London to serve his apprenticeship in the world of trade. In 1870 he established Maybrick and Co. in Liverpool with his younger brother Edwin, and began his many trips to the cotton towns of the USA. He was returning from one such trip when he met Florence.

The couple married on 27 July 1881 at St James's Church in Piccadilly and established permanent roots in Liverpool in

1884, in a house called Beechville in Grassendale Park North. During a temporary period of residence at Sefton Park, Florence got her first taste of how she was to be treated in Liverpool society. A Mrs Briggs, from whom the couple had rented their residence, had entertained more than a passing fancy for James Maybrick – and she regarded Florence as an upstart colonial. But, in general, her nationality posed no problem: the close ties between Liverpool and the southern states had long been established and, furthermore, Liverpool was a terrifically cosmopolitan city and, in the 1880s, at the height of a boom.

The Maybricks weren't grand enough to rank as the pillars of the 'currant jelly set', as the 'old' Liverpool families were called, but they were acceptable visitors at the Wellington Rooms, the city's social centre, and James was a member of the Palatine Club, the oldest and most exclusive in Liverpool. The Maybricks rarely spent more than one or two nights a week at home and on those nights would probably have company for dinner or for after-dinner drinks. The other evenings they went to card parties or dances. Every Sunday they would take a ride through the nearby woods.

By the late 1880s, the couple were leading, to all intents and purposes, a life of affluent and happy respectability with their two children, James Chandler Maybrick (known as 'Bobo' and born in 1882), and Gladys Evelyn, born in 1885. In 1887, they moved to Battlecrease House in a wealthy suburb of Liverpool. That same year, Florence may well have made two discoveries about her husband – one of which would have shaken her to the core. James had, in his years of apprenticeship in London, met a woman who had subsequently became his common-law wife, with whom he had co-habited in various parts of the country, and who had borne him five children, all of whom died in infancy. James Maybrick's second secret was that he was hooked on arsenic. It is not known for sure if Florence made these discoveries, and if they drove her to embark on an affair that year with Alfred Brierly, a cotton broker of her own age, and the man who became inadvertently responsible for her fate.

Arsenic was in common use in Victorian times, and had several applications. Both men and women used it as cures (especially for malaria), the former also used as a kind of nineteenth-century Viagra – and women used a cosmetic compound for face powder. The latter use had been common for centuries: Queen Elizabeth I had used it as part of the preparation that made her face appear white. But arsenic had another common use, one that was to prove the undoing of Florence Maybrick: chemists also used it for fly-paper.

James Maybrick had been an 'arsenic-eater' for many years and the drug was undoubtedly the reason for his increasing emotional and physical instability and, indeed, for the increasing financial problems the family began to experience. Always a hypochondriac, James worsened in 1888 and, between June and September of that year, saw the family doctor, a Dr Hooper, about twenty times. Hooper couldn't have known that Maybrick was suffering from years of drug abuse, so his condition went undetected and he prescribed his own treatment: ever-increasing doses of arsenic. Edwin Garnett Heaton, the chemist from whom Maybrick obtained his 'medicine', claimed that he came into his shop on Exchange Street East as many as five times a day to get his 'pick-me-up'.

That same spring, Florence lost her arsenic-based cosmetic

preparation and, on 23 April, bought flypaper in order to make up the concoction herself by soaking it to distil the arsenic. As mentioned in the programme, she was observed by the maid Alice Yapp. She didn't, however, make any attempt to hide what she was doing. As Alice Yapp's niece, Jo Brooks, says, 'She told her she was going to use it to cover up spots on her face.' But James Maybrick's condition had begun to deteriorate at exactly the same time, and Alice Yapp's suspicions were aroused. She talked to the family friend, Mrs Briggs (who wasn't keen on Florence in the first place), and she in turn alerted Maybrick's brothers of their suspicions. By all accounts, it seems that his brother Michael took charge of his ailing brother and saw to it that he changed his will. He did so on 25 April and Florence was all but cut out. It wasn't clear at the time – and still isn't to this day – whether it was a forgery. The original is hard to read, but contemporary newspapers published transcriptions of it.

Two days later, on 27 April, James became terribly ill and was confined to bed. Florence continued to go out and about and, on 29 April, bought a second batch of flypaper. That purchase was cited as evidence that she was poisoning her husband, but it wasn't nearly as incriminating as the next piece of 'evidence': Florence wrote a letter to Alfred Brierly and asked Alice Yapp to post it. Yapp walked to the post office with the young Gladys Maybrick. The latter was holding the letter and dropped it into a puddle. Whether Alice Yapp saw this as an opportunity to satisfy her nosiness or whether she was trying to rescue the contents of the letter will never be known, but the upshot was that she retrieved the envelope and opened it. Then she read its contents. Here are some of the words she read:

Dearest,

... I cannot answer your letter fully today, my darling, but relieve your mind of all ... fear of discovery now and in the future. M. has been delirious since Sunday, and I know now that he is perfectly ignorant of everything ... Excuse this scrawl, my own darling, but I dare not leave the room for a moment, and I do not know when I shall be able to write to you again.

In haste, yours ever.

Florie.

Alfred Brierly never read the letter but, within hours, its contents were known to the inhabitants of Battlecrease House and Florence was, in today's parlance, put under house arrest and banned from seeing her husband. After three agonising weeks of illness, Maybrick died on 11 May, 1889. Three days later Florence was arrested and charged with his murder.

The trial of Florence Maybrick took place in St George's Hall in Liverpool. The building still exists and is exactly as it was in 1889. Florence's barrister, hired by her mother, the Baroness Caroline von Rocques, was Sir Charles Russell. He had, unfortunately, endured a string of losses and, just prior to representing Florence, had fought a long, gruelling trial. At the time, he probably wasn't the best man for the job of defending Florence Maybrick. But, years later, when Florence was still serving time in prison, he was made Lord Chief Justice and continued to fight her cause. Yet at the time of her trial, Florence's cause appeared doomed: not because of the weight of evidence against her but because of the stance of the judge. Mr Justice Fitzjames Stephen, despite a long and distinguished career, was beginning to suffer from dementia or loss of reason. He was also a heavy user of opium. It was obvious from the start that he was going to be far from impartial: in his opening address to the court he described James Maybrick as a man 'unhappy enough to have an unfaithful wife'. Talk about leading the jury ...

There were two main issues the jury had to decide. Was arsenic the cause of death and, if so, had it been administered by Florence with intent to murder? The evidence presented at the trial was sketchy and inconclusive. Seven doctors testified to the cause of death being gastroenteritis, but they couldn't agree on the cause: food poisoning or arsenic?

The prosecution, however, claimed that Florence could have extracted enough arsenic from the flypapers to kill her husband. The defence countered that this could not have been the case, as there were no fibres from the paper in any of the solutions found to contain arsenic.

But by that point, it didn't seem to matter: the main issue had become Florence's infidelity, and various housemaids and other witnesses testified that she had indeed been unfaithful to her husband. And Florence did herself few favours, requesting that for the sake of the children, no mention be made of her husband's infidelities. Worse, her lawyer allowed her to make a statement to the court in which she tried to explain that she used the flypaper to make her cosmetic concoction. Her pleas to the jury, however, backfired. The statement was made towards the end of the trial, and it was the first mention from Florence of her use of the flypaper. It was, in any case, highly unusual for a defendant in a murder trial to be allowed to make a statement. The judge bluntly told the jury that her statement was a lie.

The trial ended after seven days – one of the longest of the period. Everything (except hard evidence!) appeared stacked against Florence from the start. Michael and Edwin Maybrick didn't testify to their knowledge of their brother's arsenic addiction, although both had experienced his wild moods and changes of behaviour. The judge took a mammoth twelve hours to sum up to the jury, and focused far more on Florence's infidelity than on her suspected guilt of murder:

You [the jury] must not consider this as a mere medical case in which you are to decide whether the man did or did not die of arsenic poisoning according to the medical evidence. You must decide it as a great and important case involving in itself a most highly important moral question. For a person to go deliberately administering poison to a poor helpless sick man upon whom she has already inflicted a dreadful injury – an injury fateful to married life – a person who could do such a thing as that must indeed be destitute of the least trace of human feeling. It is easy enough to conceive how a horrible woman in so terrible a position might be assailed by some fearful and terrible temptation.

The jury took just thirty-five minutes to deliver a guilty verdict. Justice Stephen donned his black cap, and Florence was sentenced to death. The Maybrick case was Justice Stephen's last. Within two years he was admitted to a private asylum for the insane.

In piecing together the story of Florence Maybrick's life, *The People Detective* wanted to track down a living descendant of hers: a potential problem, as Florence was an only child and her own two children produced no heirs. Her husband, however, had two brothers who had children, so the trail started there with the time-honoured method of looking in the Liverpool Record Office, at civil registration certificates. Several descendants were traced and David Little (an actor who uses the stage name David Maybrick), great-great-grandson of James Maybrick's brother Edwin, ended up taking part in the series.

The extraordinary amount of documented information about Florence Maybrick enabled a complete picture of her life and times to be created. Letters used as evidence in court, court records themselves and the huge amount of newspaper coverage of the trial were used in this episode. So, too, were the books written about Florence Maybrick. But the minutely detailed picture of life in the Maybrick household was largely made possible by the court transcripts themselves.

The research team was able to find out so much about James Maybrick's medical records because they are now available to the public. Medical records for individuals are subject to a hundred-year closure. Administrative records are closed for thirty years, and not many hospitals keep their older records. A few, however, have their own archives. St Barthomew's in London has records of admissions registers from 1818–1917 and clinical case notes from 1826–1920. St George's in London and Addenbrooke's Hospital in Cambridge also have their own record offices. Many hospital records have been destroyed although some surviving ones are held at local County Reference Offices.

The People Detective investigated Florence Maybrick's case partly to establish whether she would be found guilty if she were tried today. The answer has to be a resounding 'no'. Liverpool barrister Andrew Edis, who was consulted on the programme, says that the trial would have been quite different. Not only would there have been a different judge and jury (one, for a start, with women), but also the evidence would have been examined in the light of modern medical and scientific knowledge. It was the judge's attitude that most horrified Edis: 'The judge actually told the jury that he didn't understand the evidence and nor would they – but that it didn't matter! Furthermore, the absence of a fatal dose of arsenic would have been fatal to the prosecution case.'

Nowadays, they wouldn't have had any problem about the arsenic side of the equation. As Professor Robert Forrest, Britain's leading forensic toxicologist in modern poisoning cases, told *The People Detective*: 'Two grams of arsenic is enough to kill ten people. Two hundred milligrams is generally considered to be the lethal dose. The autopsy found that James Maybrick had six milligrams in him. That was not enough to kill him.'

So, if Florence Maybrick wasn't sentenced for murdering her husband, it must have been the fact that she committed adultery that convicted her. A classic story of Victorian double standards. It was quite acceptable for men to have mistresses: appalling to even consider that a wife should take a lover.

At the beginning of the trial, Florence Maybrick had been widely regarded by the public as wicked: her actions an affront to society; her guilt a foregone conclusion. People being as curious as they are, seven thousand of them passed through the public gallery during the trial and, outside the courtroom, portraits of Florence the husband-killer could be bought. Yet as the trial progressed, public opinion began to swing in favour of

Florence and, when she was sentenced to death, there was a public outcry. Even the journalists in the courtroom were shocked: 'Everybody,' wrote one, 'was surprised when dear Mrs Maybrick was found guilty.'

In 1889, Britain didn't have a Court of Criminal Appeal. Florence was doomed. Even though her trial had been a travesty and the judge well on the road to insanity, there was no system by which she could launch an appeal. Only Queen Victoria – via the Home Office – could save her. But the queen, like many others, focused on Florence's adultery and she held an extremely dim view of that. Furthermore, she wasn't known as an especially compassionate monarch and rarely pardoned criminals.

Yet so great was the public outcry over Florence's conviction that multiple petitions to the Home Secretary eventually saw the queen waver and, on the day Florence was due to hang at Walton prison in Liverpool, the sentence was commuted to life imprisonment. Florence was transferred from Walton to Woking prison, where she served the first seven years of her sentence. She was subsequently moved to Aylesbury prison, where she served a further eight years.

After Queen Victoria's death, Florence's supporters, including her mother, lobbied the authorities to end her confinement. And Florence herself asked the Home Office if she could be released into the care of a convent in Cornwall. The governor's journal notes that on Friday 25 September 1903, a sister from the convent in Truro came to visit her and, early the next year, she was finally released into the nuns' care. She spent six months preparing herself for life in the outside world and, later that year, left Cornwall and sailed back to America with her mother. She never set foot in Britain again. Nor did she ever see her children again. They chose to have nothing to do with her.

In her homeland, people clamoured to hear Florence's story. She wrote a book about her ordeal, *My Lost Fifteen Years*, and became something of a fixture on the American lecture circuit. But after two years of constantly reliving her story, she gave up and retired into obscurity. Yet without any source of income, she was obliged to seek some way to earn a living. A friend recommended her for a housekeeping position in Connecticut. She took the job, reassuming her maiden name of Florence Elizabeth Chandler. As she grew older, however, she became increasingly reclusive and, latterly, poverty-stricken. She ended her days living in a run-down shack in the small town of South Kent in Connecticut, dying on 23 October 1941, aged seventy-nine. After her death, a friend, Genevieve Austin, revealed her true identity to the press and, after years of obscurity, she once again became the notorious Florence Maybrick.

In Britain, however, Florence hadn't been forgotten. The gross unfairness of her trial helped shake the legal system to the core. A contemporary (1891) book on the trial, *Treatise on the Maybrick Case* by Alexander MacDougal, helped fuel the outcry, not just amongst the public but within the legal system. In 1907, the criminal justice system was changed and Britain's Court of Criminal Appeal was established. Had Florence been tried in that year, she would most likely have been a free woman as soon as her case was reviewed by an appellate court. Stories about Florence and her trial have continued to appear in newspapers right up to the present day.

Was James Maybrick Jack the Ripper?

The Florence Maybrick story came to *The People Detective* because series producer Jo Vale read an article published by Professor William Rubinstein in *History Today* (Volume 50 [5]). The article cited new evidence that the strongest suspect in the Jack the Ripper murders was one James Maybrick, a Liverpool cotton trader. This led to an investigation of Maybrick himself, and to the discovery of one of the most sensational trials of the Victorian era. 'The story of Florence Maybrick was straightforward,' says Jo Vale. 'Did she or didn't she murder her husband? We could follow that story easily enough once we'd found a descendant and, although we really wanted to follow the Ripper element as well, it just became too complicated. It ended up becoming a tangent to the tale of Florence Maybrick.'

Before 1992, there was no evidence to connect James Maybrick with Jack the Ripper. Yet in that year an extraordinary, sixty-three-page diary turned up in the possession of Liverpool couple Michael Barratt and Anne Graham. Handwritten and signed 'Jack the Ripper' it was dated 3 May 1889 – eight days prior to James Maybrick's death. And, in the main, it is written in a hand that mirrors Maybrick's other writings. Its discovery caused a sensation, and its authenticity is a subject that is still hotly contested amongst 'Ripperologists'.

Its provenance is also something of a mystery. Scientific tests have established that it isn't a modern forgery, and probably dates from the late nineteenth century. Yet quite how it passed to Anne Graham's antecedents is still uncertain. One theory holds that Alice Yapp (known to be light-fingered) stole it after

Maybrick's death and passed it to one Edith Formby, a family friend who had married a Graham. Another school of thought latches onto the fact that, because Florence Maybrick used the pseudonym 'Mrs Graham' after her release from prison, she had, out of wedlock and during her marriage, given birth to a son (Anne Graham's father) who took the name William Graham and that, knowing of this, Alice Yapp gave the diary to him. There is another, even more vague, theory that the diary was 'handed over in a pub' in some secret exchange. Given the unlikelihood of its exact whereabouts during its missing years ever being proven, the latter seems as good (or as bad) as any other explanation.

The fact that the diary only became public knowledge more than a century after the Ripper's crimes were committed is, obviously, grist to the sceptics' mill, yet the extraordinary contents of the document itself present an overwhelming case for Maybrick being the Ripper. Fundamentally, it contains information that any forger would have been hard-pressed to know. For example, on the police list of the possessions of Ripper victim Catharine Eddowes, an empty tin box is mentioned. The Maybrick diary makes reference to this:

I showed no fright and indeed, no light, damn it, the tin box was empty.

The full police list, however, wasn't published at the time. As still happens, in such cases, vital clues were withheld to minimise 'crank' calls: and mention of the tin box didn't come into the public domain until 1987.

If that, along with scientific testing, debunks the theory of the diary being a modern forgery, it still leaves room for the suspicion that it could have been written by a contemporary of Maybrick's – someone who knew every detail of what was happening in Battlecrease House during the years in question. The most likely contender appears to be James's brother Michael, a highly successful composer under the pseudonym 'Stephen Adams', who lived in London. Michael was the family favourite and almost certainly knew more about his brother's affairs than he ever stated in public. But why on earth would Michael go to such elaborate lengths to try to incriminate his brother? Especially as one entry in the diary reads:

> It shall come, if Michael can succeed in rhyming verse then I can do better, a great deal better he shall not outdo me ... I curse Michael for being so clever.

James had good reason to be jealous of Michael: there's no evidence to suppose that Michael was jealous of James.

The chance of the diary being a hoax seems even more remote when one considers the potential pitfalls of writing a document that accurately reported the doings of the Ripper as well as those of James Maybrick himself. For a start, all the Ripper's murders took place in London: Maybrick, whilst he travelled to the capital on numerous occasions and had a flat there, lived in Liverpool. The scope for getting facts wrong is enormous. Yet there are no inconsistencies in the diary (or any other documents) as regards the possible whereabouts of James Maybrick on the night of the Ripper murders. Every murder happened on a Friday, Saturday or Sunday – and Maybrick often spent weekends in London. And on the weekends the

Ripper murders took place, there is no record – in the *Liverpool Echo*, for example, of the Maybricks attending social events in that city. He could well have been in his Whitechapel flat in London where he lived alone, bang in the centre of the Ripper area.

But what motive would James Maybrick have had for killing prostitutes in London? The diary makes it clear (albeit in often hysterical, almost incoherent prose) that the murders were a sort of revenge on his wife for the affair she was conducting with Alfred Brierly. Almost without exception, Florence is referred to as a 'bitch' or 'whore' and Brierly as her 'whore master' or 'the bastard'.

But that gives rise to another question: why did the murders suddenly stop after 9 November 1888, when Florence was still having an affair with Brierly? A possible answer lies in James Maybrick's changing doctors shortly after that date. His addiction to arsenic was well known, yet when he consulted a Dr J. Drysdale on 19 November, the new physician treated him with homeopathic remedies and the patient appeared to improve on that and five subsequent occasions.

It's at that point the Maybrick diary refers to remorse at the murders and, vitally, to the fact that there would be no more Ripper killings. How could anyone other than the Ripper himself have known that the murderous spree had stopped? Intriguingly, the Ripper diary also has an entry stating that its author intended to stop taking huge doses of arsenic during the spring of 1889. If indeed he had taken such a step, the results could have been fatal for him.

The writer of the diary also mentions that he confessed to his wife that he was Jack the Ripper. In a letter that Florence wrote to Brierly, and which featured prominently in her trial, she states, quite out of the blue:

> ... *the tale he told me was a pure fabrication and only intended to frighten the truth out of me.*

It seems Maybrick wanted Florence to confess she was having an affair with Brierly. It also seems horribly likely that Maybrick's 'tale' was the confession that he was Jack the Ripper.

William D. Rubinstein, Professor of Modern History at the University of Wales, whose interest in Maybrick as the Ripper sparked the *People Detective* investigation into Florence, has stated that 'I am personally more than ninety per cent convinced that James Maybrick was Jack the Ripper. Both evidence and inference appear overwhelmingly to point to him. However, if it can be proved that he was definitely not the Ripper – if, for instance, irrefutable proof were found that he was in Liverpool on the night a Ripper murder was committed – the identity of Jack the Ripper remains a mystery: none of the other suspects is remotely convincing.'

Royalty, the Aristocracy and Heraldry

Despite the poverty-stricken end to her life, Florence Maybrick grew up in a world of privilege with her mother, Baroness von Rocques. Many people embark upon tracing their family history because they hope to find they're descended from aristocracy such as this: a monarch, a duke or, at the very least, a baronet. Countless people believe that, way back, somewhere in their family tree, they're going to find that aristocratic antecedent they always knew was lurking around. Several of the stories that came to *The People Detective* were along those lines – many of them from Americans. 'It's a classic American fantasy,' says series producer Jo Vale, 'to believe that you're related to the aristocracy or royalty. We had lots of those, some of which we did follow up but none of which, unfortunately, developed into a story we could use.'

The majority of people looking for a titled ancestor are going to be disappointed. Most families, let's face it, are and always have been very ordinary. Yet the desire to be well-descended isn't new. The 1700s saw the appearance of *Collins's Peerage*, whose contents were, according to modern *Debretts*, 'largely legendary'. Apparently the work was corrected by Sir Egerton Brydges in its fifth edition in 1778 and was largely accurate – apart from the insertion of Brydges' own forged ancestry.

In the Victorian era, the forging of ancestors really came into its own. The *nouveaux riches* leapt into the social scene with their new, industrial wealth and the desire for very old families. This was when genealogy began to acquire a shockingly bad reputation and charlatans posing as genealogists penned drivel for their customers, inventing ancestors until they got bored and wrote: 'The origins of this ancient family are lost in the mists of antiquity'.

The expectation that you might find a toff or two in your family tree is not, however, completely ridiculous. Up to the end of the nineteenth century, there were fifty thousand documented legitimate descendants of Edward III (1327–77), and they were people of all classes. In even a few generations, the highest in the land can descend to the lowest. And vice versa: of the sixty-four g.g.g.g. grandparents of the Queen Mother, there were dukes, earls, clergymen – and a plumber and a toymaker.

Royalty, in fact, is a great example of, if not botched genealogy, then at least gilding the lily. The great unbroken line (if you skip over the Commonwealth) of the British monarchy is, depending on which way you look at it and which era you go back to: Danish, Greek, French and, just possibly, English.

They're helped, of course, by the fact that, historically, members of royal families had no need for surnames: they were known by the countries or territories they ruled over (Queen Elizabeth II still only signs herself 'Elizabeth'). They may have had other Christian names, but only one other name mattered: that of the dynasty to which they belonged. Those names tended to change when the reins of succession were taken by a rival faction within the family. Henry V (1413–22) was a Lancastrian, but his successor was the Yorkist Edward IV (1422–61). After the Yorkists came the Tudors whose succession passed through the female line to James I (1603–25), who was a Stuart. So it isn't true that kings and queens always take the name of their father's line. James I's father was Lord Darnley, who was of little importance and who was, in fact, English. The 'Stuart' name was his mother's Scottish inheritance.

But things started going really awry in 1714 when Queen Anne died leaving no heirs and the net had to be cast fairly wide before a distant cousin, the Hanoverian George I, was deemed fit to rule England (the fact that he didn't speak English was clearly irrelevant). Hanoverians ruled until Queen Victoria decided her children should bear their father's name, so, on her death in

1901, the dynasty changed to Saxe-Coburg-Gotha. That didn't last long; in 1917, anti-German feeling was rife throughout Britain, so George V changed it to the safe and very English-sounding 'Windsor' (after the castle).

Queen Elizabeth II, while maintaining that name for the dynasty, decided that her children should bear the surname Mountbatten-Windsor as a gesture to Prince Philip, whose surname was Mountbatten. Except that it wasn't: Mountbatten had originally been the German 'Battenberg', although Prince Philip's own father had actually been Prince Andrew of Greece and was, in fact, Danish. Confused? That's only the potted version. Still, it's a pretty good indication of how adroit the royal family has been keeping their throne: 'Adapt or Die' should be their motto. Perhaps it is – especially in light of events in the 1990s.

Despite the ramifications of the name changes and dynasties, it's unlikely that any of us are going to be able to trace our pedigree to royalty. As genealogist Steve Thomas says: 'If you're related to royalty, you're going to know about it.'

Oddly enough, one of the *People Detective* contributors, Charlotte Sainsbury, who followed the trail of her ancestor, James Chalmers, to Papua New Guinea, *is* descended from royalty. She had an authenticated family tree tracing her line back to James V of Scotland – but, as she explains, 'on the wrong side of the sheets'. Still, it's better than most of us can do.

The aristocracy have, like the royal family, been great name changers. This is usually because of the various titles held by a family and granted to them over the years or centuries. A duke's son, for instance, will be the earl of somewhere-else while his daughter will be lady something-different (usually the family name). Given that there are a great deal more aristocrats than there are members of the royal family (of whatever dynasty), it's not unlikely that some of us may be able to work back to them. In view of the number of ancestors everyone has, it's not impossible that the pedigrees of the nobility may touch on your family tree at some point. That doesn't, however, mean that you will be noble. Nor does it mean that you will be entitled to a coat of arms.

A huge number of people, especially those who contact a professional genealogist, do so in order to embellish their family tree with a coat of arms. They're likely to be extremely disappointed. If you find a titled ancestor who had the right to bear arms, this doesn't mean you have the same right. This is because there is no such thing as a coat of arms for a surname; coats of arms belong to individuals. In continental Europe, the story is slightly different. Familial heraldry – as opposed to individual heraldry – exists too and means that all male descendants of the original grantee bear exactly the same coat of arms.

Given that heraldry is such an interesting part of genealogy and is a sort of 'shorthand of history', it's worth considering the bare bones of the subject here. Debrett's *Guide to Tracing Your Family Tree* says that: 'There is probably more nonsense and misunderstanding about heraldry than about any other aspect of genealogy and family history.' It goes on to say: '[its] origins date from the eleventh century and arose from the need for personal identification on the battlefield and through the use of seals on legal documents.'

There is, however, another school of thought that claims Debrett's is talking a lot of nonsense: that heraldry as we know it dates from Charlemagne's time and that it was useless as a means of identification in battle because of the general carnage, mud and blood of the battlefield.

In reality, it probably doesn't matter where it originated because it all leads back to the same thing: the ancient use of symbolic devices for the purposes of identification (which, in layman's terms, is what heraldry is). Ancient Egypt possessed devices by which civil and military authority was recognised; early Roman standards carried symbols for identification, and biblical mention is made of it in *The Book of Numbers* 2:34: 'And the children of Israel ... pitched by their standards and so they set forward, every one after their families, according to the house of their fathers.'

The point, for genealogists, is that heraldry as we know it – a system of devices portrayed on a shield – developed all around Europe in the twelfth and thirteenth centuries. Identification in tournaments appears to have been their major function, although arms *were* worn on the battlefield. A display of status, wealth and ownership was another consideration. Arms were also used for decorative purposes. At first, they were appropriated and displayed without approval from anyone, but, probably as early as the twelfth century, their use and the granting of them was brought under the aegis of the crown. Heralds originally officiated at ceremonies and became experts in recognising the arms that knights wore on their shields and the crests on their helmets. Because of this expertise, and because coats of arms were hereditary, the heralds were later sent out by the monarch to regulate the right to use them and to grant new arms to people who had been elevated to the peerage or granted a knighthood. These jaunts were called Visitations, and they happened roughly every twenty or thirty years, from 1530–1686.

In 1484, the heralds were granted a charter of incorporation by Richard III and were also given premises in London which became known, and is still known although the location has changed, as the College of Arms. Officially, it is called the Corporation of the Kings, Heralds and Pursuivants of Arms, and still regulates the granting of arms to this day, although the right to bear them is officially controlled by the Earl Marshal (a hereditary position held by the Dukes of Norfolk) on behalf of the queen.

Armorial bearings are hereditary. For any person to have a right to a coat of arms, they must either have had it granted to them or must be a legitimate descendant in the male line from a person to whom arms were granted or confirmed in the past. Furthermore, a coat of arms belongs to an *individual* or, increasingly, to a corporation. They do not belong to surnames or to families. And it's worth pointing out that the expression 'coat of arms' actually refers to the shield part of the arms. The correct term for arms is an 'achievement' – and it usually consists of a shield, helmet, crest and maybe two supporters (like the lion and the unicorn supporting the arms of the queen), a blazon (a written explanation of the shield) and possibly a family motto.

The really intriguing aspect of a full achievement of arms is the amount of information it divulges. There are many books on the subject that explain the full meaning of arms and heraldry but, basically, the various designs, images and layouts of, in particular, a shield, can reveal information about several families from whom an individual is descended. It will also reveal whether the person to whom the arms belong is an heir or a subsequent son. A crescent, for example, is the symbol of a second son whilst the symbol of the fleur-de-lis belongs to a sixth son.

A common misconception is that a 'family crest' is the same as a coat of arms. This is not the case. The crest, the symbol at the top of a full achievement, is a specific part of the whole and, although it does pertain to a family, it shouldn't, strictly speaking, be used unless members of that family have the right to bear arms. Someone with that right is referred to as being 'armigerous'.

If you think you have the right to bear arms by descent but don't have proof, you'll have to pay for the privilege of finding out. In England and Wales, your first port of call should be to approach the Officer in Waiting at the College of Arms with details of your personal ancestry. He will then begin a search within the records of the college and, if necessary, outside the college to extend the search. In Scotland, a similar approach should be made to the Lord Lyon and, in Ireland, to the Chief Herald of Arms.

If you find that you don't have the right to bear arms, you're highly unlikely to have any joy seeking proof elsewhere. Heralds have the weight of at least five centuries of experience behind them, and they developed scientific genealogical methods at an early stage. One herald, William Dugdale (d.1686), Garter King of Arms (all heralds have peculiar titles), was one of the greatest pioneers of genealogical research in England. What's more, the records and collections at the College of Arms are extensive – and unique.

Many of the duties of the heralds have disappeared over the

centuries, but they still carry out some spectacular ceremonies. Every June at Windsor Castle, the procession and service of the Sovereign and Knights Companion of the Order of the Garter is held and, in November, they officiate at the State Opening of Parliament. They are also involved in coronations and state funerals. They can be easily identified by their distinctive medieval uniform, known as a tabard, embroidered on the front, back and sleeves with the Royal Arms.

One last thing: if you can't find any grandeur in your ancestry, you can always buy it in the form of a manorial title. The sale of such titles has recently become a voguish way for out-of-pocket aristocrats to raise capital and for the newly-wealthy to attach status to their riches. One of the best known aristocrats to do this is Earl Spencer, brother of the late Princess of Wales: he has auctioned various minor lordships he inherited in order to help fund the maintenance of Althorp House, his Northamptonshire stately home. And famous buyers of such titles include: the boxer Chris Eubank, reputed to have paid around £50,000 for the Lordship of Brighton; conductor André Previn, who became Baron of Tirerrill in County Sligo for a rumoured £30,000, and Nicholas Graham, founder of the giant US underwear label Joe Boxer, who – appropriately – owns the Manor of Balls in Bedfordshire.

But what do you get for your outlay? Nothing very much, is usually the answer. The purchase of a manorial title doesn't enable you to call yourself 'Lord' or 'Lady', nor to bear a coat of arms. In the majority of cases, nothing tangible comes with the title, although some include, for example, fishing rights. Others may come with tiny pockets of land which, in reality, are legacies of some peculiar feudal ruling and grant you the ownership of, say, all the grass verges in a village. Scottish manorial titles tend to bring greater novelty prizes such as the right to wear an ermine robe and to be escorted by two pipers everywhere you go.

But, historically, and from the point of view of the genealogist, manorial titles are extremely interesting. In medieval England, a manor was usually an estate comprising the 'big house', a village, a church and some land. The lord of the manor was responsible for the management and administration of the estate and, astonishingly, the system continued until well into the nineteenth century. This means that manorial records can often be a treasure house of information about local life in the area. Regular courts would be held by the steward of the manor on behalf of the lord. These courts mostly concerned themselves with the buying, selling, inheriting and leasing of land, but they often dealt with what we would now call local bylaws and, sometimes, with the trying of petty criminals or settling of small claims. Many documents relating to these transactions survive in local record offices but, crucially for the genealogist, many of them are still in the hands of the lord of the manor. Some information may well still be locked in a private deed box or with a local solicitor. Ownership of a manorial title, then, gives you the right to these documents or, if they are in an official record office, the right to access them.

Many people buy these titles for precisely this reason: they're not interested in the snob value of a title but in the historical associations. Many manorial titles also bring with them membership of the Manorial Society of Great Britain, a loose affiliation of manorial lords which meets once a year. And some manors are bought for romantic or nostalgic associations with a particular place. When Earl Spencer sold the Lordship of Wimbledon for the staggering sum of £191,000, for example, the anonymous purchaser was rumoured to be tennis legend Boris Becker.

The College of Arms

'Everyone here is bonkers in some way,' says Windsor Herald. 'I like to think I'm less bonkers than most.' He is, in fact, not at all bonkers, but a rather sensible ex-company secretary and chartered accountant which is, he freely admits, highly unusual for a herald at the College of Arms. 'Most of us started as research assistants and worked our way up.'

Windsor (you address heralds by their titles) explained how he became a herald: 'I started off one notch up from a research assistant as a Portcullis Pursuivant on a salary of £13.95 a year. Then you do that *Kind Hearts and Coronets* business and kill off all the people ahead of you to become a herald – on £17.80 a year. Kings of Arms get more: around £20. And the Garter King of Arms gets £49.07.'

So he's not in it for the money, then. But Windsor Herald's sense of history is as healthy as his sense of humour. This is clearly a job he relishes, even if he does have to supplement his income from the world of finance. He skipped being a research assistant because he had already worked on a dictionary of medieval arms, which gave him vital heraldic military knowledge, and he subsequently became Windsor Herald 'because it was the next title that became available' (on the previous Windsor's death).

Career progression is along the 'dead men's shoes' line – and dead men are the herald's speciality. 'Our main task is establish pedigrees so that we can establish a right to bear arms granted to an ancestor. But, remember, there's no such thing as a family coat of arms. They're for individuals. And if you've established the right to bear arms you have to place your pedigree on record here within our jurisdiction.' That jurisdiction covers the whole of the UK and the Commonwealth except Scotland and, now, Canada. Establishing one's right, however, can be enormously difficult and time-consuming. 'One of the most complicated I've done was a chap who came in claiming that he thought he was a baronet. I had to prove that about 114 people between him and the last baronet, up and down the line, had died without legitimate issue. It took me about three years – but he's now a baronet.'

Many people, says Windsor Herald, are extremely surprised at the volume of material held at the College of Arms. 'We're a sort of human Cruft's: vast numbers of pedigrees. We also do a lot of biographical research: not just certificates and dates of birth but regiments they served in and other information to put the flesh on the bones of pedigree-tracing.' Having such a vast database of pedigrees means that there will invariably be some sort of crossover at some point. 'I had somebody in here last year,' continues Windsor, 'who was just about to start on his pedigree and wondered if we had anything. I was able to show him that we already had his pedigree on record from the time of Elizabeth I right up to 1896 ... it killed off his summer activity in one fell swoop. But, actually, he was thrilled.'

And there's a pretty serious side to all this. All succession claims have to come through the College of Arms and the body advises the Home Office on baronetcy claims and the Crown Office on peerage claims (the rolls of baronets and peers being held respectively within those two organisations). If, then, there is any question about the legitimacy of the claims to a title, the College of Arms is consulted and the matter resolved.

Further Information

Sources for Heraldry and the Aristocracy
College of Arms
Queen Victoria Street
London EC4Y 4BT
Tel: 020 7248 2762
www.college-of-arms.gov.uk

Genealogical Office of the Republic of Northern Ireland
3 Kildare Street
Dublin 2
Tel: 00 353 1 603 0200
www.heanet.ie

House of Lords Record Office
House of Lords
Westminster
London SW1A 0PW
Tel: 020 7219 3074
www.parliament.uk

Institute of Heraldic and Genealogical Studies
79–82 Northgate
Canterbury
Kent CT1 1BA
Tel: 01227 768 664
www.ihgs.ac.uk

Scottish Record Society
(Postal enquiries only)
Hon. Secretary
Scottish History Department
Glasgow University
Glasgow G12 8QQ

Publications
Debrett's *Peerage*
Burke's *Peerage*
Dictionary of National Biography

SIGNIFICANT DATES
for Family Researchers

1066	Norman Conquest
1086	Domesday Book compiled
1190	Julian calendar introduced into England. The Julian year began on 25 March and finished on 24 March the following year. The months January to March of any given year therefore came *after* the months April to December. This system lasted until the introduction of the present system (the Gregorian calendar) in Scotland in 1600 and in England and Wales in 1752
1290	Edict of Expulsion stated that all Jews in England were to be baptised, banished or put to death
1348	Black Death
1476	First English printing press set up by William Caxton in Westminster
1484	College of Arms founded
C16th	Reformation spread across Europe, giving rise to Protestant and Evangelical churches
1534	Church of England founded under Henry VIII
1536	Act of Union between England and Wales (Henry VIII was Welsh)

1538	Parish registers introduced in England and Wales
1553	First parish register introduced in Scotland
1559	Acts of Supremacy and Uniformity made it illegal to celebrate a Catholic mass in England and Wales
1572	First Huguenot influx into Britain
1585	First unsuccessful English settlement founded on Roanoke Island off North Carolina by Sir Walter Ralegh
1600	Gregorian calendar introduced in Scotland
	Formation of the East India Company that, effectively, governed India
1601	Poor Law Act in England and Wales rationalised the system of relief to the poor
1607	First successful English settlement in America founded at Jamestown, Virginia
1611	Authorised version of Bible published
1617	Beginning of transportation of convicts to America and the West Indies
1620	Voyage of the *Mayflower*
1634	First official Irish parish registers
1652–8	Monarchy abolished and Cromwell made Lord Protector
1656	Edict of Expulsion revoked by Cromwell, leaving Jews free to enter England
1659	First unofficial Irish census listed those with titles to land
1660	Monarchy restored
1670	First settlers arrived in Canada
1707	Act of Union between England and Scotland

1708	Protestant refugees allowed to be naturalised without a private Act of Parliament
1732	Parish registers started to be compiled in English rather than Latin
1752	Gregorian calendar introduced in England and Wales
1753	Lord Hardwicke's Marriage Act tightened up marriage laws. All marriages (even Nonconformist) to be performed in an Anglican parish church or chapel and properly recorded in the register. Only Quakers and Jews were exempt
1770	Captain Cook landed at Botany Bay, Australia
1775–83	American War of Independence
1776	Catholic Relief Act ended persecution of Roman Catholics and legalised the celebration of mass
1785	*Daily Universal Register* founded. Three years later, it changed its name to *The Times*
1787	Transportation to Australia began
1790s	New Zealand settled by whalers and traders. First free settlers arrived in Australia
1798	Irish Rebellion
C19	Highland clearances in Scotland
1801	First official census in England, Wales and Scotland. It was just a head count and contained no names, addresses or any other information
	Act of Union between Britain and Ireland
1804	First steam engine demonstrated
1805	Ordinance Survey, Britain's mapping agency, began making maps on a scale of one inch to one mile

1806	Beginning of colonisation of South Africa
1807	Abolition of slave trade
1821	First official Irish census
1823	Establishment of prisons with the amalgamation of county jails and Houses of Correction
1829	London Metropolitan Police force founded
	Catholic Emancipation Act allowed Roman Catholics to participate in public and political life
1834	Poor Law Amendment Act introduced workhouses
1835	First recorded photograph of a person made by Frenchman Louis Daguerre
1837	Civil registration of births, marriages and deaths introduced in England and Wales
1838	First Public Record Office established
1841	Census in England, Wales and Scotland recorded names, addresses, ages and occupations
1845	Civil registration of non-Catholic marriages introduced in Ireland
1845–50	Great potato famine in Ireland killed a million people and sparked an exodus to the colonies and America
1851	Census in England, Wales and Scotland recorded relationships within households and places of birth
1855	Introduction of civil registration of births, marriages and deaths in Scotland
1857	Matrimonial Causes Act made divorce in England and Wales possible through a civil court. Prior to its passing, divorce was only possible through a private

Parliamentary Bill. The Act meant that husbands could divorce wives for adultery but wives had to prove both adultery and cruelty. This didn't change until 1925. In Scotland, divorce for ordinary people was possible in court from 1560

1858   Britain declared India a crown possession

1864   Civil registration of births, marriages and deaths began in Ireland

1869   Disestablishment of the Church of Ireland

1873   First national Ordinance Survey map of the whole of Britain published

1874   Births and Deaths Act made it illegal not to register births and deaths

1882   Suicide victims allowed to be buried in consecrated ground (although suicide remained a crime)

Married women legally allowed to own property (prior to this date, all their possessions belonged to their husbands)

1905   Aliens Act limited immigration

1911   Society of Genealogists founded

1914–18 First World War

1914   Aliens Registration Act passed, requiring all foreigners over the age of 16 to register with the police

1918   Women over the age of 30 given the vote

1922   Ireland divided into Northern Ireland and the Republic of Ireland

Dublin Public Record Office destroyed by fire

1926	Adoption of Children Act introduced formal, legal documentation into the process of adoption. Previously, adoption was often done on an informal basis, requiring no written evidence
1928	Voting age for women lowered to 21 (the same as men)
1929	Age of marriage with parents' consent raised to 16. Previously it was 12 for girls and 14 for boys
1939–45	Second World War
1947	India became independent
1948	Establishment of the National Health Service
	Citizens of British colonies given British nationality, which led to an influx of immigrants from the West Indies
1962	Immigration of citizens from the colonies restricted to skilled workers and their dependants
1969	Age of voting reduced to 18
1974	Foundation of the Federation of Family History Societies (FFHS)
1975	Adopted people over the age of 18 allowed to apply for their birth certificates
2002	Census returns for 1901 released to the public

THE
MONARCHY TIMELINE

William I	1066
William II	1087
Henry I	1100
Stephen	1135
Henry II	1154
Richard I	1189
John	1199
Henry III	1216
Edward I	1272
Edward II	1307
Edward III	1327
Richard II	1377
Henry IV	1399
Henry V	1413
Henry VI	1422
Edward IV	1461
Edward V	1483
Richard III	1483
Henry VII	1485
Henry VIII	1509
Edward VI	1547

Mary I	1553
Elizabeth I	1558
James I	1603
Charles I	1625
The Commonwealth	1649
Charles II	1660
James II	1685
William III & Mary II	1689
Anne	1702
George I	1714
George II	1727
George III	1760
George IV	1820
William IV	1830
Victoria	1837
Edward VII	1901
George V	1910
Edward VIII	1936
George VI	1936
Elizabeth II	1952

USEFUL ADDRESSES

Achievements
79–82 Northgate
Canterbury
Kent CT1 1BA
Tel: 01227 462 618
www.achievements.co.uk

Association of Genealogists & Record Agents
29 Badgers Close
Horsham
West Sussex RH12 5RU
For a list of reliable genealogists and record agents send £2.50 sae (UK) or 6 IRCs (overseas)

Association of Scottish Genealogists & Record Agents
PO Box 174
Edinburgh EH3 5QZ
www.asgra.co.uk
For a list of reliable genealogists and record agents working in Scotland send a first-class SAE (UK) or two IRCs (overseas). Alternatively, the list is published on the web site.

Association of Professional Genealogists in Ireland
c/o The Honorary Secretary
30 Harlech Crescent
Clonskeagh
Dublin 14
Eire
www.indigo.ie
For reliable genealogists and record agents in Ireland, send two IRCs.

Barnardo's Head Office
Tanners Lane
Barkingside
Ilford
Essex IG6 1QG
Tel: 020 8550 8822
www.barnardos.org.uk

Bodleian Library
Broad Street
Oxford OX1 3BG
Tel: 01865 277180
www.bodley.ox.ac

British Library
96 Euston Road
London NW1 2DB
Tel: 020 7412 7000
www.bl.uk

British Library Newspaper Library
Colindale Avenue
London NW9 5HE
Tel: 020 7412 7353
www.bl.uk

British Telecom Archives
Holborn Telephone Exchange
268–270 High Holborn
London WC1V 7EE
Tel: 020 7492 8792

British Telecom Internet Directory
www.bt.com/phonentuk

Child Migrants Trust
28a Musters Road
West Bridgeford
Nottingham NG2 7PL
Tel: 0115 982 2811

Church Mission Society
The Archivist
Partnership House
157 Waterloo Road
London SE1 8UU
Tel: 020 7928 8681

Church of England Record Centre
15 Galleywell Road
London SE16 3PB
Tel: 020 7898 1030
www.church-of-england.org

College of Arms
Queen Victoria Street
London EC4V 4BT
Tel: 020 7348 2762
www.college-of-arms.gov.uk

Corporation of London Records Office
PO Box 270
Guildhall
London EC2P 2EJ
Tel: 020 7332 1251
www.corpoflondon.gov.uk

Edinburgh Central Reference Library
George IV Bridge
Edinburgh EH1 1EG
Tel: 0131 242 8060
www.edinburgh.gov.uk

Edinburgh City Archives
Department of Corporate Services
City of Edinburgh Council
City Chambers
High Street
Edinburgh EH1 1YJ
Tel: 0131 529 4616

Family History Centres
There are almost a hundred Family History Centres in the
British Isles, all of them branches of the library of the Mormon
Church in Utah. Below are the addresses of British
Headquarters and the Distribution Centre. The e-mail address
is: www.familysearch.com

Genealogical Society of Utah
British Headquarters
185 Penns Lane
Sutton Coldfield B76 1JU
Tel: 0121 384 2028

LDS (Church of the Latter-Day Saints) Distribution Centre
399 Garretts Green lane
Birmingham B33 0UH
Tel: 0121 785 2200

Family Records Centre
1 Myddelton Street
London EC1R 1UW
Tel: 020 8392 5300 (general enquiries)
0151 471 4800 (certificate enquiries)
www.familyrecords.gov.uk

Federation of Family History Societies (FFHS)
(No current address but phone 0161 797 3843 for information)
www.ffhs.org.uk

FFHS (Publications) Ltd
Units 15 & 16
Chesham Industrial Centre
Oram Street
Bury BL9 6EN
Tel: 0161 797 3843
www.familyhistorybooks.co.uk

Folklore Society
Warburg Institute
Woburn Square
London WC1H 0AB
Tel: 020 7862 8264

French Protestant Church of London
8–9 Soho Square
London W1V 5DD
Tel: 020 7437 5311

Genealogical Office of the Republic of Northern Ireland
2 Kildare Street
Dublin 2
Tel: 00 3531 603 0200
www.heanet.ie/natlib/

General Register Office (England and Wales)
PO Box 2
Southport
Merseyside PR8 2JD
Tel: 0151 471 4800 (general enquiries)
        0151 471 4816 (to order a birth, marriage or death
certificate)
GRO indexes are also held at the Family Records Centre, London
www.statistics.gov.uk

General Register Office of Northern Ireland
Oxford House
49–55 Chichester Street
Belfast BT1 4HL
Tel: 028 9025 2021/2/3/4/5/
www.nisra.gov.uk/gro

General Register Office of the Republic of Northern Ireland
Joyce House
8–11 Lombard Street East
Dublin 2
Tel: 00 3531 635 4000
www.groireland.ie

General Register Office for Scotland
New Register House
Princes Street
Edinburgh EH1 3YT
Tel: 0131 314 4433
www.gro-scotland.gov.uk

Guild of One-Name Studies
Box G
14 Charterhouse Buildings
Goswell Road
London EC1M 7BA
www.one-name.org

Guildhall Library
Aldermanbury
London EC2P 2EJ
Tel: 020 7332 1868/1870
www.cityoflondon.gov.uk

History of Advertising Trust
Hat House
Raveningham Centre
Raveningham
Norwich NR14 6NU
Tel: 01508 5486623

HM Commissary Office
Sheriff Court House
27 Chambers Street
Edinburgh EH1 1LB
Tel: 0131 247 2850

HM General Register Office
HM Register House
Princes Street
Edinburgh EH1 3YY
Tel: 0131 535 1352

HM Land Registry
Lincoln's Inn Fields
London WC2A 3PH
Tel: 020 7917 8888
www.landreg.gov.uk

Home Office
Departmental Record Officer
50 Queen Anne's Gate
London SW1H 9AT
Tel: 020 7273 3000
www.homeoffice.gov.uk

Home Office Immigration and Nationality Directorate
3rd Floor
India Building
Water Street
Liverpool L2 0QN
Tel: 0151 237 5200
www.homeoffice.gov.uk/ind

House of Lords Record Office
House of Lords
Westminster
London SW1A 0PW
Tel: 020 7219 3074
www.parliament.uk/pa/ld/ldhome/htm

Huguenot Society of Great Britain and Ireland
Huguenot Library
University College London
Gower Street
London WC1E 6BT
Tel: 020 7380 7094

Imperial War Museum
Lambeth Road
London SE1 6HZ
Tel: 020 7416 5000
www.iwm.org.uk

Institute of Commonwealth Studies
28 Russell Square
London WC1B 5DS
Tel: 020 7862 8844
www.sas.ac.uk/commonwealthstudies

Institute of Heraldic and Genealogical Studies (IHGS)
Northgate
Canterbury
Kent CT1 1BA
Tel: 01227 768 664
www.ihgs.ac.uk

Irish Genealogical Research Society
c/o The Irish Club
82 Eaton Square
London SW1W 9AJ
Tel: 020 7235 4164

Jewish Genealogical Society of Great Britain
PO Box 13288
London N3 3WD
www.jgsgb.ort.org

Lambeth Palace Library
Lambeth Palace Road
London SE1 7JU
Tel: 020 7898 1400

Liverpool Record Office and Local Studies Centre
Central Library
William Brown Street
Liverpool L3 8EW
Tel: 0151 233 5817
www.liverpool.gov.uk

London Metropolitan Archives
Corporation of London
40 Northampton Road
London EC1R 0HB
Tel: 020 7332 3802
www.cityoflondon.gov.uk/archives/lma

Ministry of Defence Army & Navy Records Centre
Bourne Avenue
Hayes
Middlesex UB3 1RF
Tel: 020 8573 3831
www.mod.uk

National Archives of Ireland
Bishop Street
Dublin 8
Tel: 00 3531 407 2300/2333
www.nationalarchives.ie

National Archives of Scotland
HM General Register House
Princes Street
Edinburgh EH1 3YY
Tel: 0131 535 1314
www.nas.gov.uk

National Library of Ireland
Kildare Street
Dublin 2
Tel: 00 3531 603 0200
www.heanet.ie/natlib/

National Library of Scotland
Department of Manuscripts
George IV Bridge
Edinburgh EH1 1EW
Tel: 0131 226 4531
www.nls.uk

National Library of Wales
Department of Manuscripts and Records
Penglais
Aberystwyth
Ceredigion SY23 3RU
Tel: 01970 632 8000
www.llgc.org.uk

National Maritime Museum
Park Row
Greenwich
London SE10 9NF
Tel: 020 8858 4422
www.nmm.ac.uk

National Registry of Archives
Quality House
Quality Court
Chancery Lane
London WC2A 1HP
Tel: 020 7242 1198
www.hmc.gov.uk

North of Ireland Family History Society
c/o Graduate School of Education
Queen's University Belfast
69 University Street
Belfast BT7 1HL
www.nifhs.org

Office of the Chief Herald of Ireland
Genealogical Office
1 Kildare Street
Dublin 2
Tel: 00 3531 603 0200
www.heanet.ie/natlib/herald/

Post Office Archives and Record Centre
Freeling House
Phoenix Place
London WC1X 0DL
Tel: 020 7239 2570

Principal Registry of the Family Division
(for probate offices and divorce registers)
First Avenue House
42–49 High Holborn
London WC1V 6NP
Tel: 020 7936 7000

Public Record Office (PRO)
Ruskin Avenue
Kew
Surrey TW9 4DU
Tel: 020 8392 5200
www.pro.gov.uk

Public Record Office of Northern Ireland
66 Balmoral Avenue
Belfast BT9 6NY
Tel: 028 9025 1318
www.proni.nics.gov.uk

Religious Society of Friends (Quakers) Library
Friends House
173–177 Euston Road
London NW1 2BJ
Tel: 020 7663 1135
www.quaker.org.uk/library

Republic of Ireland Probate Office
Four Courts
Dublin 7
Tel: 00 3531 888 6174

Royal Naval Museum
Buildings 1–7
College Road
HM Naval Base
Portsmouth PO1 3LJ
Tel: 023 9283 9766
www.royalnavalmuseum.org/

School of African and Oriental Studies (SOAS)
(for missionary records)
Library Archives
Thornhaugh Street
Russell Square
London WC1H 0XG
Tel: 020 7898 4180

Scottish Genealogical Society
Library and Family History Centre
15 Victoria Terrace
Edinburgh EH1 2JL
Tel: 0131 220 3677
www.sol.co.uk/s/scotgensoc/

Scottish Record Society (postal enquiries only)
Hon. Secretary, Scottish History Department
Glasgow University
Glasgow G12 8QQ

Society of Genealogists
14 Charterhouse Buildings
Goswell Road
London EC1M 7BA
Tel: 020 7251 8799
www.sog.org.uk/

Trinity College Library
College Street
Dublin 2
Tel: 00 3531 677 2941
www.tcd.ie/library

Ulster Historical Foundation
Balmoral Buildings
12 College Square East
Belfast BT1 6DD
Tel: 028 9033 2288
www.ancestryireland.com

Addresses Overseas
Australia
National Archives of Australia
Queen Victoria Terrace
Parkes Place
ACT 2600 Canberra
Tel: 00 61 2 6212 3900
www.naa.gov.au/

National Library of Australia
Parkes Place
ACT 2600 Canberra
Tel: 00 61 2 6262 1111
www.nla.gov.au

Society of Australian Genealogists
Richmond Villa
120 Kent Street
Sydney
NSW 2000
Tel: 00 61 2 9247 3953

New Zealand
National Archives of New Zealand
PO Box 12–050
Wellington
Tel: 00 64 4499 5595
www.archives.govt.nz

New Zealand Society of Genealogists Inc
PO Box 8795
Symonds Street
Auckland 1035
Tel: 00 64 9525 0625
www.genealogy.org.nz

Central Registry of Births, Marriages and Deaths
PO Box 31 115
Lower Hutt
Tel: 00 64 4570 6300

South Africa
Genealogical Society of South Africa
Suite 143
Postnet X2600
Houghton 2041
www.rootsweb.com/~zafgssa/eng

National Archives of South Africa
Private Bag X236
24 Hamilton Street
Arcadia
Pretoria 0001
Tel: 00 27 12 3235300

United States
Immigrant Genealogy Society (IGS)
PO Box 7369
Burbank
California 91510–7369
Tel: 00 1 818 348 6444
www.feefhs.org/igs/frg-igs.html

National Archives and Records Services
700 Pennsylvania Avenue, NW
Washington DC 20408
Tel: 00 1 202 501 5400
www.nara.gov/

National Genealogical Society
4527 17th Street North
Arlington
Virginia 22207–2399
Tel: 00 1 703 525 0050
www.ngsgenealogy.org/

INDEX